Ray,
To our journeys

SHOOTING at the Navy Yard

One Survivor's Memoir

Laurel Myers

Copyright © 2014 Laurel Myers.

All rights reserved. No part of this book may be reproduced, stored, or transmitted by any means—whether auditory, graphic, mechanical, or electronic—without written permission of both publisher and author, except in the case of brief excerpts used in critical articles and reviews. Unauthorized reproduction of any part of this work is illegal and is punishable by law.

ISBN: 978-1-4834-2102-5 (sc)
ISBN: 978-1-4834-2101-8 (e)

Library of Congress Control Number: 2014919737

Because of the dynamic nature of the Internet, any web addresses or links contained in this book may have changed since publication and may no longer be valid. The views expressed in this work are solely those of the author and do not necessarily reflect the views of the publisher, and the publisher hereby disclaims any responsibility for them.

Any people depicted in stock imagery provided by Thinkstock are models, and such images are being used for illustrative purposes only.
Certain stock imagery © Thinkstock.

Lulu Publishing Services rev. date: 01/15/2015

*To those who cannot be with us today, through
no fault of their own, we honor them.*

*To the Americans who helped on that terrible day, Captain Theodore
of Building 200 on the Navy Yard where we were mustered for the
majority of the day; he made the best of a bad situation and opened all
five floors to his unexpected guests, helping everyone who asked, while
all of his employees dug deep into their drawers for food to help us
make it through the day. To the Red Cross for feeding us after having
gone though a long day with only the food that was shared with us, yet
with many of us not having eaten since 0630. Finally, to Ubercars;
providing free rides to those of us who were stunned and waiting for the
next step, a way to get to our cars in commuter lots, we owe thanks.*

*To those who are with us, our families, near and far, love
them like today is the last day you will ever see them, because
you may walk out the door in the morning heading to work
and truly, never see your loved ones again in this world.*

*To my husband and children who support me throughout my ordeal;
I love you all.*

PREFACE

This book is a first-hand account of the shooting at the Navy Yard from someone who was just yards away from the shooter when he fired the first shot from his shotgun. It tells of the initial chaos and questions going through people's minds, the disbelief of the state of affairs; that there was someone shooting a weapon inside a secure building, a building people were led to believe was secure in all ways, not just as a means to protect classified documents.

Whether you are interested in the beginning of the shooting, comparing the events as they unfolded as told by an eye-witness to those of the media, or the timeline of events to and from extraction and beyond; and present a frightening view to readers of encounters with the assailant that won't be provided by news media or the investigative reports. This book reveals interesting information from a survivor's point of view. The information provided will make you question the definition of secure. It will make you question the information provided by news outlets.

The Purpose of this Publication

There may be many excellent books forthcoming on the subject of the Washington Navy Yard shooting that occurred in building 197, but

I expressly wrote this book as a means of coping with the devastating events that took place on September 16, 2013, which I'll never forget. For me personally, I felt that writing this book was important for the following reasons:

- We should never forget the 12 victims who found themselves in the wrong place at the wrong time through no fault of their own
- Many workers in Building 197 as well as a number of first responders performed acts of heroism that should not go unmentioned
- A number of news reporting agencies just plain got the story wrong from the beginning and the facts of actual events needs to be told
- Although a lot of procedures and systems worked as planned during the shooting, there were a number that simply did not work and should be brought to light
- The more individuals who write about this event, the better historians can piece together the bigger picture of what actually occurred on that day
- Insights of my experience may lead to better emergency planning for the future
- Finally, I wrote this book as an assignment by my counselors and therapists to speed my physical, emotional, and mental recovery

CONTENTS

Chapter 1	911. What is Your Emergency?	1
Chapter 2	Reliving the First Shots	17
Chapter 3	Relaying the Sounds	24
Chapter 4	The Evacuation	36
Chapter 5	Where are they?	46
Chapter 6	The Heroes	52
Chapter 7	The Sanctuary	59
Chapter 8	Getting Home	73
Chapter 9	I Need Help!	78
Chapter 10	What were They Thinking?	86
Chapter 11	Memorial Services	97
Chapter 12	A Caring Program	107
Chapter 13	Treatment Trials	123
Chapter 14	Leadership Response	135
Chapter 15	Planning for a Future Disaster	144
Chapter 16	Additional Thoughts	158
Chapter 17	Epilogue	173

Glossary 179

CHAPTER 1

"911. What is Your Emergency?"

"911, what is your emergency?"

"There are shots being fired in Building 197 on the fourth floor!" I replied. Then I identified myself and where I was situated on that floor. I told the operator I was going to find out where the shooter was located and where he was heading. She stopped me and told me to stay put and to listen to where the shots were coming from, then let her know in which direction the sounds of the shots were coming from so she could relay that information to the police when they entered the building.

In order for readers to picture locations more easily, I need to describe the building layout. Building 197 has a west and east side, and three sections. Though these sections have a preponderance of cubicles, they also have blocks of offices, on both the east and west sides; with purple walls on the north end, orange in the middle and blue on the south end of the building. The color coding of the section walls makes it easier to navigate such a large building. My desk is located in a cubicle in the center section, referred to as the Orange Section, on the fourth floor of Building 197 (see Figure 1). This section of cubicles also contains part of the department associated with quality of parts as deliverables in contracts. My cubicle is the last cubicle at the end of a cubicle hallway containing rows of four cubicles along both sides. It is also just a few steps from the atrium banister that overlooks the center of the first floor atrium of the building. There is a second floor atrium that extends up to the skylight in the roof between the orange and blue sections of the west side of the building. The east side of the building was added after the original factory was built and contains the elevators that run from the first to the fifth floors.

Building 197 used to be a factory that built 16 inch guns for ships. When the factory wasn't needed anymore, a front was added to the building. The factory side is the west side of the building and the newer section is the east side. The numbers of the offices are preceded with a floor number and the letter W or E for West or East. For example, office 2W-1600 would be on the second floor of the West side (the factory side) of the building. Now to explain the last four numbers. The building also has blocks of offices situated on the north and south sides and one block of offices in the middle of the building. These blocks are color coded so employees and authorized visitors alike can find specific rooms. The walls on the south side, closest to the Anacostia River, are painted blue, the middle section is orange, and the north side is purple. These colors are associated with a numbering system. The purple side has rooms numbering from 1000 to 1999, the orange section rooms number from 2000 to 2999 and the blue section numbers from 3000 to 3999. When combined with the east or west side of the building, the room number has an E or W in front, and depending on the floor, from the first floor to the fifth, there will be a number from 1 to 5 in front of the letter. If someone provided directions to go to room 2W-3560, one would first go to the second floor, then head to the west side, the old, or factory part of the building. This part of the building is the blue colored section, and has the 3000 to 3999 numbers. Once on the second floor and in the blue section of the older, or factory side of the building, the search begins for the office or cubicle numbered 3560.

It's a matter of narrowing down the area in which the search needed to begin. Now for an explanation of my location. The number of my cubicle was 4W-2118. This meant my cubicle was on the fourth floor of the west side of the building, the older part of the building. The four digits were the actual cubicle number and told people where my cubicle was located on the fourth floor. The fact that the number was in the 2,000's told people my cubicle was in the center of the building in the west wing. The remaining three digits were the actual cubicle number, number 118. The layout of the cubicles on this floor had my cubicle sitting next to the banister that overlooks the fist floor by the cafeteria.

It was about 08:17 a.m. when I got the operator on the line. I dragged myself under the free-standing part of my desk where my computer monitor sat. One look around told me that this was a stupid choice for a hiding place so I crawled backward toward the vertical file section of my desk. This area under my desk was dark because it was against the lower bookshelf under the desktop and not easily seen from the hallway. However, this location was against the outer wall and forced me to sit against the back wall of the cubicle. I could push against the back wall that butted against the adjacent cubicles on the other side and any movement against the wall would reveal my position. However, since this section of my desk was against the back wall of my cubicle, it afforded me a better chance of not being noticed if the shooter happened to only glimpse in my direction.

The location of my cubicle allowed me to hear everything that was going on around the walls of the atrium. Being stationed on the fourth floor also allowed me to identify where sounds were coming from, whether above or below. I didn't have to worry about sounds coming from the fifth floor because that floor is locked and requires a Common Access Card (CAC) to gain access.

I pulled my desk chair in front of me to hide my silhouette. I also dragged my carry-all bag under the chair in an attempt to camouflage my body. Then I took off my shoes and put them on top of my bag as high as I could pile them. I made a feeble attempt to make this pile as tall as possible because I was wearing a brightly-colored pink jacket and it would be easy to spot me behind my open weave chair. There wasn't much use in taking the jacket off either because under that I was wearing a lively pink blouse with black lace. Even with the black lace, the pink outfit made me stand out. I cowered back as far as I could into that dark recess under my desk.

My cubicle was built with four cloth sides, the sides interrupted only by a doorway, whereas the cubicle to my west, across from me, has only two and a half sides. The tops of my cubicle walls also extend upward with an extra two feet of glass for more privacy. The extra wall and glass at the top provides me the privacy I need to conduct employee counseling and workforce planning meetings. However, this privacy worked both ways. I couldn't hear discussions my employees were having in the walkway because the sound came to my ears muffled and garbled, but I could hear what people were saying down in the atrium. The echoes of the noises from down there on the first floor took no time at all to rise to my floor, and I could hear them clearly, as they bounced off the ceiling above and came back down.

These privacy features now worked to my advantage in that they afforded me an opportunity to talk on the phone to the 911 operator and not be heard in nearby cubicles or in the open areas around my area on the fourth floor. Conversations from any of the other cubicles can be heard as far away as the first floor in the atrium, especially if they are near the balcony to the atrium. I knew this because my office mates often let me know afterward that my meetings at our table near the atrium banister were heard down on the first floor. For this reason, we were always cognizant of what we discussed and who we spoke of during our meetings.

There also was nowhere to hide in the open cubicle across from me. It was fortunate the employee who typically occupied that cubicle was teleworking that day. She didn't have to frantically try to find somewhere else to hide, knowing that her cubicle would not afford her much seclusion. Our contractor had just called about an hour ago to let me know he was just getting over a migraine and would be late, so I knew I didn't have to worry about him either. I only had three other employees to worry about: one down my aisle, one co-worker stationed in the cubicle next to mine, and my supervisor. I didn't know the fate of my supervisor. So, as her second in command, it fell to me to find out the fate of her group in addition to mine. I did know the manager of the intern program was teleworking this week so she was safe. The budget analyst was here already and I didn't know where she was. My early arriving employee was here at work too, but I didn't know where she was either.[1]

---

[1] In a statement by Washington D.C. Police Chief Parlave, "We have not determined there to be any previous relationship between Alexis and any of the victims. There is no evidence or information at this point that indicates he targeted anyone he worked for or worked with. We do not see any one event as triggering this attack."

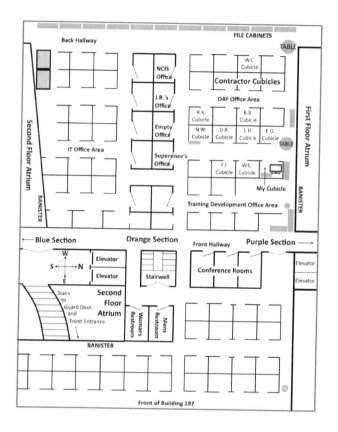

Figure 1. Layout of the Center Section (Orange Section) of the Fourth Floor in Building 197—just outside my cubicle area is the walkway that overlooks the atrium to the first floor.

While recounting to myself the wherabouts of the employees in our area, I heard the gunman say, "Fourth floor," and then something in too low a voice to be understandable, followed by a shot. Then he pumped his weapon. I knew then that he either had a cartridge-fed pump action weapon or shotgun and that he didn't need long between shots to get another round into the chamber. That meant there wasn't time to get to him, even if someone was brave enough and close enough to try.

After his first utterance "Fourth floor, mumble" and shot, the gunman repeated the pattern again after a momentary pause. It appeared to me he was after someone who worked on the fourth floor just because of what he was saying before he discharged his weapon each time.

It seemed like it was only a few minutes since I punched in the numbers 911 on the telephone and began talking to the operator when the police arrived and began entering the building. I remember thinking that they certainly responded quickly, even if it was from the DC Metropolitan Police Department instead of the Navy Yard police, as I had expected. As I spoke with the 911 operator I was puzzled because the operator was asking me if the shots were in a building on the Navy Yard. I answered, "Yes," expecting her to already know this fact. When I first started working at the Navy Yard, I remember being told that if I used my desk phone to dial 911, the call would go directly to the Navy Yard Police Department, but if I used my cell phone, the call would go to the DC Police Department, thus delaying the response. Yet this operator acted like she didn't know where we were in the DC area. So, I made sure to identify the location of the building on the Navy Yard.

I let my mind dwell on this conundrum for just a little while because that would mean that even from our desk phones, calling 911 at any time in the future would be routed to the DC Metropolitan Police Department instead of the Navy Yard Police Department, creating delays in response times during emergencies. I filed that away in the back of my mind for later reference.

The operator asked me how I knew the sounds were shots. How does one tell someone that the sound of a gunshot is immediately identifiable, and the sounds of shots can pretty well tell you whether it's a large or small caliber weapon being used? I heard the weapon being pumped instead of cocked to be reloaded. This pretty much narrowed down the number of weapon types. I let her know that I knew the sound of the weapon firing and could identify it as a pump action weapon. That, combined with the operator's ability to hear the shooter again yelling "Fourth floor" followed by additional unintelligible words as he fired another shot helped convince her I wasn't some crazed woman calling because I'd heard some books slamming to the floor. The operator continued to ask questions about how many people were in my section. I answered and gave her their names. I knew this was for later identification, should the need arise, and that didn't set well with me.

My story doesn't begin with the operator, but really begins with the first two "bangs." They weren't what you would think of as shots from a gun. They sounded muffled. I put together the details from the sounds I heard with the pattern of the killings in the order I recollect them, and later balanced them against co-workers' accounts as we walked through the building after the evidence was collected and we were allowed to return for some of our work and personal effects.

This all started with two loud sounds, but not those of loud gunshots; more like sounds of metal striking metal. When I first heard these sounds, I thought there were people on the first floor of the atrium putting tables out and dropping them. That is how loud these sounds were, and that's the closest description of the sound heard; and the sound that came to our attention. Later on, as I pondered on the sounds and what could have made them when the shooter was the only person making any kind of loud sound, I had to admit it sounded to me as if the shooter was assembling his weapon and had to slam metal pieces into each other, or was loading shells of some kind into his weapon then slamming a magazine into place. It was more of a loud metal-on-metal banging sound and not the typical gunshot sound heard during the rest of the event.

The third noise I heard sounded distinctly different, more definitely like a live round was being fired. It was close, too close. To me it was obviously a gunshot that I heard. I later found out that the first two muffled sounds I heard were indeed gunshots, but I was hearing them through two sets of offices, and two hallways away. Apparently, the shooter had assembled and readied his weapon in the men's restroom located in the east wing of the fourth floor. Investigators proposed that it was about 08:20 a.m. or so when he likely exited the restroom and headed toward the atrium that opens to the second floor. The first shot we heard was at 8:15 a.m. exactly. The investigators were wrong. I remember looking up at the clock on the wall and comparing it to the clock on my computer when I heard the shots that sounded like tables banging. That is how I know when the shooting started. It was about 8:14 a.m. when he likely exited the restroom and headed toward the blue section, stopping well short of the atrium that opens to the second floor. He was still in the orange section, but if he kept going, and stayed in the hallway instead of walking into the cubicle area, he would have passed the open second floor atrium and entered the blue section. However, he stopped short of the second floor atrium, probably because he saw movement of people there. He most likely turned to look toward the movement and therefore toward the open area over the second floor atrium.

It was at this point he fired one shot killing a man and a woman the man was trying to shield. The two were evidently entering a cubicle at the far end of the first row of cubicles in the wide expanse of cubicles and were caught off guard. The shooter then turned 180 degrees and headed back to the IT side of the orange section where he shot one of the supervisors who came to see what the noise was and made it all the way to the east side of the floor before being felled. He killed her in the bathroom hallway he'd just left after preparing his weapon. It was probably at the shooting of this victim that I first heard the shooter yell, "Fourth floor," and then something unintelligible in a lower voice followed by the sound of the shot. The IT supervisor investigating the noise was most likely the first person addressed in such a way before being shot. No one mentioned anything about the shooter speaking or yelling anything as he fired his first shot at the man and woman he killed, and I heard no echoes of his voice.

I believe that after killing the supervisor, instead of heading toward the blue section, the shooter continued down the hallway between offices and cubicles of the IT area of the orange section before yelling "Fourth floor," saying something unintelligible, and then shooting and killing the man whose cubicle was the first one on the end of the aisle facing the offices. These two shooting episodes were separated by a period of a few moments of silence. The man in the end cubicle was most likely the second person targeted by the shooter in such a manner; with the "Fourth floor," something unintelligible spoken, and then being shot. It was the second time I heard the shooter yell out the "Fourth floor" phrase before shooting the shotgun.

After the shooter fired what seemed like the third shot, I saw my supervisor, Jill, step out of her office and ask, "What the heck is going on here?" as she headed down the hallway between the kitchens toward the IT section. Wilma, a coworker, just happened to be standing at Jill's office door at the time. No sooner had Jill spoken her words heading around the corner to that hallway when she apparently saw the shooter, then she gave out a scream, turned and ran back toward her office where Wilma grabbed her and pulled her into the office, closing the door behind them. I later found that inside the office, Wilma hauled Jill off to the side of the door behind the bookshelf because they weren't sure if the door was locked and hiding behind the side of the shelves seemed the most sensible thing to do. After a period of silence, both of them moved under the desk and as they did so, Wilma pushed in the lock on the door to make it harder for the shooter to get in. They both sat there until the shooter was eliminated and they thought the way was clear for them to open the door to the next person who knocked.

I heard later that as the chaos escalated, Jill's excitement level increased to the point Wilma had to tell Jill to "be quite!" I know Wilma wouldn't normally say something like that to our supervisor, but she was under duress and needed to be sure there was no noise coming from their hiding place under that desk! Be quiet turned out to be a nice interpretation of, "Shut up, Jill," the words actually used by Wilma several times.

When the next shot rang out, it sounded to me like the shooter was in the back hallway near the IT offices. I half expected him to walk up the hallway along the offices on our side of the orange section; the sound of the weapon seemed that close. I later found out he was in the east IT hallway, crossing into the west IT hallway. After killing the man at the end of the cubicle aisle in the IT section, the shooter continued down the IT hallway along the orange section and turned into the kitchen hallway where Jill saw him. He went past the kitchens, and came toward my area. I no longer heard the shooter uttering "Fourth Floor" again as he meandered around. As he headed toward our area through the kitchen hallway, ominously, he spied my employee, Nina. She was coming down the hallway past Jill's office toward her cubicle in an attempt to get under her desk for cover. He was close. She didn't get to her desk, but saw the shooter as he began raising his weapon, lifting it in one measured, purposeful movement, as if in slow motion. He continued raising the weapon in an arc when he finally had it pointed directly at her.

I could hear Nina pleading for her life, telling the shooter that she had a son at home and she was all he had to raise him. As Nina later articulated to me, "I helplessly watched the weapon coming straight up at me while gazing into the shooter's eyes as I pleaded for my life." She said she saw that awful look that made her realize the shooter was really going to kill her. "I looked into his eyes and I knew he was going to shoot me." That realization must have hit her like a lightning bolt because at the moment he pulled the trigger, she said she dropped and turned to run as he fired his weapon, then bounded toward Wilma's cubicle, escaping the spray of shotgun pellets by mere inches. BANG! That shot was deafening. It rang out across the cubicles and down my spinal cord to the cramps in my feet. Even I could hear the shotgun pellets pepper the metal in the walls of the cubicles. I felt the concussion of that shot and it was all I could do not to scream out. As Nina ducked, the shooter attempted to follow her with his weapon. Luckily the shooter had to reload and as terrified as I was, I started thinking it was a good thing that even pump action shotguns have to be reloaded. If not for that, I fear he would have tried to shoot her a second time. From only four feet away, his initial shot ended up smashing through the glass of the cubicle window behind Nina as he over-corrected his aim.

A chilling thought went through my mind when I heard the shot. From only four feet away, what were the chances he missed her? Oh Lord, please make him miss!" I thought of the horror of it all; how her son would find out later that his mother was taken from him, and in such a callous manner! The inhumanity of that sent tremors through me! How could he just shoot her after she told him about being the only person left for her son? Now her son would grow up without a mother and he wouldn't be able to enjoy those mother-son outings she spoke of; the field trips with his class, the visits to the museums, the trips to shows, the battlefield site visits. They did so much together and had so much planned to do yet.

After firing his last round in Nina's direction, he reloaded his weapon, at which time he turned and went toward the back hallway, and then headed toward the banister overlooking the first floor atrium.

However, my thoughts and observations of the shooter were interrupted by the sound of running footfalls headed in my direction. My God, he shot Nina and now he's headed in my direction at a run!

Shooting her must have given him a real high. It's as if he was operating at super-speed! And now he's headed toward me! I started shaking uncontrollably! If I was wearing boots, I would be quaking in them! As it was, I was quaking in my stockings under my desk! I just knew I was next. I crowded as far back into my little dark space as I could and tried hard to make myself as small as I could. Hearing what I thought was the shot that took Nina out crushed my heart! Now I had an empty feeling in my chest. She was such a trooper, such a strong woman, a force to be reckoned with. She could stand up to her leadership with arguments they couldn't refute. It was awesome watching her work to influence our leadership based on facts alone and leaving out the emotion that others used to drive decision-making. I feared I would never get to see that happen anymore, and she won't be standing up to anyone anymore. We won't be partners for what's right in training anymore! Damn that man!

The footsteps ran down to Wilma's cubicle next to mine first, and then bolted around the cubicle walls into mine. I was holding my breath, praying that I remained concealed and unseen. I was shocked to see it was Nina flying into my cubicle. She scared the hell out of me because I thought she was dead and the footfalls I heard were those of the shooter coming into my area looking for me!

Unbelievably, the shooter had missed her! Focusing in the present now I begin to put the pieces of the puzzle together. He apparently had to take time out to reload his weapon. This presented her with the opportunity to escape before he could cock his weapon again after reloading. The sight of Nina took me back in disbelief! If I wasn't already on the floor I would have fallen on the floor! I couldn't believe my eyes. I almost fainted when another shot rang out. Was he coming after her? As I was trying to move my camoflage out of the way to grab Nina, I was painfully aware that no one else followed her into my cubicle. Where did the shooter go? I found out later where; he turned and went toward the back hallway, down the last row, and to the banister overlooking the first floor atrium.

Russ sits in the first cubicle of that last row toward the back hallway and was on the phone, but I found later, as he saw the end of the weapon coming around his cubicle area he hung up and ran toward the atrium. Knowing he wouldn't make it around the end of the row, he jumped over the wall of the cubicle behind his and hid under the desk next to the file cabinet, trying to make himself as small as possible. At the time he didn't realize the shooter shot at him. That was the shot I'd heard. As the shooter went to the banister to look for targets, Russ tried to remain still, but the shooter looked at him as he turned and walked back past the row of cubicles to the hallway. Russ pleaded, "Please, don't shoot me." The shooter continued on past the cubicle leaving Russ untouched. Kammie wasn't in the office that day. Her cubicle was the last one down that aisle. There is no way to know for sure what would have become of her, had she been there; that is where the shooter stood to look over the balcony.

Just after Nina left my cubicle, I heard another blast, only this time it was louder than the last one; I feared the worst for Nina. I was certain that this time the shooter had hit his mark. Why did she go back out there? She was safe back here and she left, heading to what *I* was sure was certain death! What made her leave? I last saw her alive a moment ago, and I was thinking that if I'd been faster, I could have saved her! Why, oh why couldn't I have been faster at grabbing her, and dragging her down under my desk with me? WHY? I was shaking at the thought that she ran to her death and I could have saved her if only I was a little faster. Now all I could think of was Nina lying dead in the hallway—blood oozing from her lifeless body just moments after I saw her. God, why didn't she turn around while looking for a place to hide so she could see me, and then duck under the desk with me? She would have been safer than running out in the path of the shooter.

Thinking about this really upset me. It hurt so much to think I would never see her; never talk to her again.

Joel, the supervisor of an adjacent department, was meeting in his office with one of his employees. Joel's office is just two doors down from Jill's office. If it wasn't for that timely meeting, Susie, one of Joel's employees, would have been in eminent danger because she would have been in the cubicle on the opposite side of Russ's cubicle and would have been the first person seen by the shooter as he walked down the hallway. At the time, I didn't even know if Wade from their group was working that day. He is situated along the back wall of cubicles along the path the shooter took to the balcony. It was Wade's cubicle that Russ jumped into and hid in when he saw the shooter's weapon coming past the side of his cubicle.

The shooting seemed to subside after what seemed like 15 minutes to me. It was clear the shooter had moved down to the floor below us, but his shots could still be heard from the open atrium area. This provided an opportunity for those who were fortunate enough, to get out of the immediate area. I found out later that when Nina ran to the front of my row of cubicles, she saw the shooter leave toward the front stairs, so she knew she would be safe going toward the back stairs by heading between the cubicle rows and offices. By the time the shooter was downstairs, Nina and Russ had already exited down the back stairs along with Reba, whom I didn't even know was present in her cubicle on the fourth floor during the shooting spree. I remained behind on the telephone with the 911 operator providing information on the shooter's whereabouts.

Wilma and Jill stayed put for fear of running into the shooter and ending up dead. Both decided to wait until there was some definitive sign that it was safe to exit the office. I found later they heard the shooter come by their door and try the handle several times during this event. Eventually, after what sounded like a gunfight of epic proportions, a SWAT team came around and tried the doorknobs of all the doors in an attempt to open each; the objective; to find a second shooter, or survivors. It was then that Wilma and Jill opened their office door. They figured that the shooter was acting alone, or with only one accomplice, so if the gunfight meant the shooter was dead, and there was more than one person at the door, it had to be the police and not the shooter, his accomplice, or both. As they went downstairs to the first floor via the rear staircase, our NCIS agent grabbed them and escorted them to a safe room, one of our training rooms. Since there might still be an accomplice of the shooter roaming the building, it wasn't safe to go too far without a police escort. Luckily, the police remained on the fourth floor. Our NCIS agent had an office right next door to Joel's, and we invited him to many of our celebrations so he knows all of us well enough to recognize us from afar and we know him well enough to listen to him when he says to get into a room and lock the door as Jill and Wilma did.

The shooter's path was varied as he weaved around our area, and then again as he came back into our area. I could tell the general area where he was by the sounds of his shots as he moved through the building, and that was my purpose in staying on the phone with the operator; to assist in providing the shooter's movements to her so she could provide them to the police.

CHAPTER 2

Reliving the First Shots

"Call 911! Call 911!" a man running between the row of offices and cubicles yelled out as he rushed on his way to the exit away from the noise. I was contemplating a quiet, but busy Monday work day when all the commotion started.[2] I still had work left over from Friday. I was in the middle of planning my next step on a policy letter change when my concentration was disturbed by the ringing phone. It was Fred, my group's contractor assistant, calling to let me know he was feeling ill and would be late coming in to work. I told him to wait until he was feeling better before coming in. I let him know that it was alright to take his time even though there was still a lot of work to do in preparation for an upcoming event. I knew he was conscientious and would be in as soon as he was feeling better. At least Nina was already at work so we could do a little planning together before we were overtaken by other tasks. Monday morning was off to a busy start and

---

[2] Surveillance video released by the FBI on that morning shows Aaron Alexis pulling his rental car into a garage, walking into the building with a bag casually slung over his shoulder and later, skulking down a corridor with a shotgun.

the pressure was on to get things done. So much would happen this morning and in such a short amount of time.

Then, out of the clear blue, a loud noise, and then another loud noise. My first thought was, "What are they doing in the atrium now?" I wasn't prepared for the next sound, "BANG!" That was *not* the sound of banging tables or dropping of chairs downstairs in the atrium. That was on our floor and just a couple of cubicles away from mine. What in the world other than a gun would make that loud of a sound? It had to be a gun being fired![3]

At the first sound, my supervisor, Jill, popped out of her office and said, "What in the world is going on?" She headed toward the sound. There was no mistaking where the sound came from; the puzzling part to her had to be what was making that noise? It sounded like a gunshot, but we all knew that couldn't be the case because we're in a secure government building, after all. In my mind, there was no way a gun could get in. Then I heard my supervisor scream and run. Those unmistakable footfalls of her running were easily recognizeable; we were so familiar with the sound she made when walking and running up and down the hallway. Although her running on our floor was unmistakable, her pace was different than her normal running sound. This sound had a faster, almost desperate sound to it. Then in a moment,

---

[3] A timeline issued by the FBI shows Alexis started the rampage on the building's fourth floor and then moved down to the third and first floors. He ultimately returned to the third floor, where he was killed around 9:25 A.M. While FBI Director James Comey said there's no evidence that Alexis shot down into the atrium despite earlier accounts from witnesses at the scene, I find it difficult not to believe an eye witness account. Even when I think of a shotgun spread, I immediately think of the clay pigeons used for target practice and find that the shotgun is the best method to ensure a "kill" when targeting someone. The "kill shot" to the cafeteria doorway is only 50 to 60 feet from the fourth floor atrium; an easy shot to make when unhurried. . . and this, one of the first shots was unhurried.

there was no more running sound, I heard no other sound from her. This meant that either she ducked into an office or exited the hallway in order to get out of the building. This set off alarm bells in my head.

The footfalls of the man running down the hallway yelling, "Call 911! Call 911!" on his way to the closest exit were clear as a bell to me. They were so clear; in fact, I could tell he was heading from the kitchen hallway toward the front hallway by the diminishing of those footfall sounds as he continued to run away from the noise. By this time, I was already dialing the 911 operator. There was something in all of this commotion, from that first loud "BANG," that indicated something was wrong, and that we were experiencing gunfire in our "secure" building, on our floor, and not far away from me.

As I was dialing, my mind was recalling the shootings that occurred in Colorado and Conneticut. I was thinking to myself, "These things don't happen here. They happen in defenseless schools or movie theaters where they are least expected, and to children who aren't in secure buildings. This just can't be happening here and now. It has to be a drill. This isn't happening." The feeling was so ethereal I couldn't make a connection between the shot I heard and the fact that this could possibly be affecting me. It felt like I was living in a fairy tale and could step out of it anytime I wanted. As I'm thinking about this fairytale, the world seemed to be passing in slow motion. I could picture myself in a dream, and expected to wake up any minute.

The sounds around me were strange, the running footsteps, the shuffling of people as they ran through the doors to the stairs in the front hallway, the thumps of feet as they heavily hit the floor running from our area to the Purple Section at the north endof the fourth floor. Every sound I heard felt to me as if I was hearing them from a tape being played in slow motion. It just didn't sound real. The sound of people's footfalls running from the cubicles behind me, each time a person ran by, came to my ears as if done in slow motion. All of those thoughts were going through my head, and all at the same time. The things that go through your head at a time like this are not what you'd think of normally happening. No thoughts of "I'm going to die." My mind was focused on tracking where the shots were coming from and who was shooting. GOD, I wonder if the shooter is heading in my direction. Where is that 911 operator? Finally, the operator answers the phone.

I was driving on automatic after hearing that first gunshot. I dialed 911 because I shouldn't be hearing gunshots. When it dawned on me; when I finally realized that what was happening was real, the operator answered the phone. When I told her there were shots being fired, she seemed hesitant; almost like she didn't believe me. As she asked how I knew they were gunshots, I began sorting through the chaos around me and the feelings I had that this couldn't be happening. I had to explain to her that I knew what a gunshot sounded like before she would believe me. I now realized that since I hadn't starting running by now, I was in dire danger.

With the realization of the moment starting to set in and the sound of shots heading around our area, combined with the prior verbal "threats" made by the shooter made me feel like I was in a far off land experiencing a make-believe fantasy gone wrong. But, now I somehow felt safe because the shooting sounds were becoming more far off, as if they left our area. The feeling was short-lived because the shooting sounds were coming back. I pulled my chair toward me as I crunched myself back into the dark space between my vertical file and lower bookshelf. Then I pulled my briefcase under my chair to cover that space and piled my shoes on top of the briefcase. Anything I could do to make my bright-pink jacket less visible. The sensation that I was in danger again returned and stayed with me this time. I told the operator what the shooter was saying just before he shot his weapon, and the direction he was headed. When he headed back in my direction, I told her he was coming back and stopped talking so I wouldn't attract attention to myself. As he passed by our area, I told her he was headed toward the front of the building. I was fully aware that the building had enough nooks and crannies for the shooter to hide, which would impede the police search in their efforts to find him, if I didn't use the shots and his footfalls as guides to place him at specific areas in the building for them.

I asked the operator how many others she had on the line from our building and she said I was the only person from our building talking to a 911 operator. I expressed amazement and decided then that I would stay on the line to help as much as I could. I counted shots and provided directions for her to relay to the officer standing next to her as a means to assist the police in finding the shooter. Her officer would be relaying any information I provided to the team inside the building. During a pause in the shooting, my mind began to drift and I began to wish I could call my husband to tell him how much I loved him. Then I would be prepared to die if the shooter should find me. Without my cell phone readily available, this was not possible. I really yearned to talk to my husband right about now. I was so frightened I didn't even think to have the operator relay a message to my husband.

Shots being fired brought me back to reality and away from thinking of that stupid policy keeping me from having a cellphone with me at my desk so that I could call my husband, if needed.

All of those thoughts flooded my mind, and all at the same time. The things that go through your head at a time like this are not what you'd think of normally happening. No thoughts of "I'm going to die," and, "The things I'll miss because I will be dead," went through my mind. My mind was focused on tracking where the shots were coming from and who was shooting. GOD, I wonder if the shooter is heading in my direction?

I dutifully counted the shots and relayed the number and location to the operator. There were several sounds of individual shots fired. Now that reality set in, I was thinking that each shot I heard like that had to be fired at a person. Now I'm conjecturing; if he's in that area, who is he after? Why is he going in that area? Did someone there upset him for some reason? I was still thinking that he must have a problem with someone on the fourth floor or he wouldn't be yelling, "Fourth floor," and then something unintelligible before he fired each of those two shots I heard earlier. Now it occurs to me; he had to be an employee or contractor because if he wasn't, he would have had an escort.

I heard the police confront the shooter several times, but the encounters always ended up in exchanges of gunfire and not in his capture. During each encounter I overheard, it seemed like the police would tell the shooter to stop, then they would identify themselves as police and command him to put his hands up. On each occassion the shooter simply ignored their commands and then fired at them. As a result, the police would return fire, but the shooter would run away and continued to elude them. I was thinking to myself, "Do they actually think the shooter would just come out with his hands up, and surrender just because they told him to?" And another thought, "if they have a clear shot at him, which they must if they can see him to give him the "Stop..., hands up," warning, why don't they just take the shot instead of repeatedly telling him to stop?"

After the first encounter, I asked the operator if the police got the shooter. So I asked her the same thing again after the police had their third encounter with the shooter. Even after three tries at "Stop, police, put your hands up!" the police expected the shooter to stop his shooting response to their demand! They must have thought he would get tired of hearing the demand and actually put his hands up! Well, I heard this happen three separate times and there is no doubt in my mind that this whole incident could have ended much earlier if one of two things happened. The shooter would have no one to shoot at if everyone managed to get out in time not to be targets, which one knows is impossible; or the police learned from the first encounter with the shooter that the protocol they were using was't going to work and changed their tactics to be more aggressive after finding out what the response would be during that first encounter with the shooter.

The police held their ground and continued using their protocol, possibly in the hopes of capturing the shooter alive for questioning. Meanwhile, more innocent victims were massacred. The police will insist their protocol must be followed, I'm sure. However, if a protocol is not working, then change is in order, and quickly. It was with some trepidation that I asked the 911 operator about the status of the shooter after hearing the third demand from the police to put down his weapon. She tells me to hold on and the line goes silent while she asks someone about the outcome of the most recent encounter the police had with the shooter. Where is that operator? How long does it take to find out if the police got that shooter? After all, this is the third time they confronted him. Finally, she answers the phone.

CHAPTER 3

Relaying the Sounds

"Oh great, someone set off the fire alarm!"

While I was on the telephone, that tell-tale shrill racket sounded throughout the building. I couldn't help making that statement to the operator. She could hear the noise over the phone. Why would someone set off the fire alarm? Now I had to talk to the operator over the din of the alarm and announcements to "leave by the nearest exit," all the while trying to discern the shooter's location. It was easy to hear the shooter walking around when it was silent in the building, but now there was an alarm blaring, and on top of the alarm, there was the continuous announcement to exit the building. I told the operator it would be nice if the police could turn off the alarm so I could hear where the shooter was and be more accurate in pointing the police in his direction. She didn't say anything to that; telling me she wasn't aware of any connection between the police action and the alarm. I assumed the police turned on the alarm to confuse and irritate the shooter. It certainly irritated me! The fire alarm kept blaring and the announcement to, "Exit the building using the nearest exit," kept repeating.

Knowing the shooter was on the same floor and could come near enough to me to find me, there was no way I was going to pay attention to the evacuation announcement. I wasn't going to risk getting killed trying to obey a nonsensical command. I'd rather get reprimanded than die following the instructions given to us over the loudspeaker. To top it all off, after about 25 minutes, another announcement came on that said, "Shelter in place—do not move until police come to evacuate you." It was then that I knew for sure I was right in not moving!

He's back on the fourth floor! This time the shooter was just around the corner in the front hallway near the stairs. I heard some women screaming, but strangely no shots rang out. I thought that odd. If he was going around shooting and shot at Nina, why didn't he shoot any of those women? Oh my God! I heard the commotion of someone that sounded as if he was trying to get away. The shooter just shot again, and the commotion stopped. My God! That shot sounded as if it came from the maintenance contracting section; the area right next to us. The shooter just shot someone else! Jesus, was it Rick this time? It was from that direction. Oh my God, Oh my God! I couldn't hear if he said "Fourth floor" again because the fire alarm was so doggone loud!

Suddenly, it sounded like the police found him because I heard their command to him. They had to have tracked his shots even as I was giving directions to the 911 operator. They must have triangulated him by crossing my directions with the sounds we were hearing from him. I heard the police identify themselves to the shooter and command him to put his hands up. Then I heard gunfire ring out from both directions; shots came from the shooter and return fire from the police. Then there was silence. I asked the operator if they got the shooter. After a pregnant pause, she said I needed to stay where I was because they hadn't gotten him yet.

Building 197 used to be a factory that built the 16-inch guns for naval battleships. The cranes and girders are still in place, as an acknowledgement of the building's history, with numerous offices constructed around them. The cranes form the focal point of these atria. This setup with the girders still in place, provides many places for the shooter to hide and all it takes is a little exploring to see the many nooks and crannies that can be used as hiding places.

A number of times I heard the police go over to the Purple Section of the fourth floor. I had the feeling they must have thought he wasn't there anymore. Yet I knew there were so many hiding spots he could have his choice of any number of them and would be well hidden. He very easily could have gone from behind one set of file cabinets to another without the police ever noticing him.

At one point, as I was talking to the 911 operator, it sounded like the police eventually found the shooter on the first floor. The echoes of police activity and chaos were dramatic across the atrium. However, there was no way I was going to go down to the first floor to find out if it was over. I felt I had such an advantage being on one of the upper floors. I was sure that if the DC police were in the building, they would be on the fifth floor searching for the shooter from the vantage point offered above by the atriums. The one problem with the fifth floor is that an ID is required to gain access and only some IDs allow entrance. DC police wouldn't have known that, but the Navy Yard police would. In my mind that is why I think the shooter started his shooting spree on the fourth floor instead of the fifth floor—he couldn't get up there without the proper ID.

I began to put the pieces of the puzzle together a little at a time but still couldn't make sense of it all. To me, the shooter was after someone on the fourth floor because that is what he said before he shot some people. This puzzle piece was about the vantage point offered by the height of the floors, and why the shooter would pick our floor to start his carnage. It all started making sense to me now; after the fact. The shooter probably wanted to begin his shooting as high as he could get and my floor was as high as he could have gone to do as much damage as he could. Of course, I can logically think this out now, but during the shooting there was no thinking—there was just reaction. The 911 operator kept me busy counting shots and telling her the direction from which they were coming as best as I could. There were several more shots and once again there was the oft-repeated warning, "Police, put your hands up" followed by more gun shots, return shots from police, and then nothing more for a while. The sounds were deafening, like a surround sound movie flick. Except this was no movie. I stayed crouched down, terrorized by the thought of the shooter coming back to my area.

I was totally exhausted from squatting under my desk in the same position. I so wanted to get up and see where the shooter was at a time he was focused on the police and not me. Luckily, the 911 operator talked me out of it; however, I did put the phone down to reposition to a more comfortable and advantageous position where I wasn't sitting on only one side. This allowed me to sit in a position that let me put my head out past my chair so I could get a better idea from where the sounds of the shooter's shots were coming.

I didn't realize how stiff I was until I tried to move. Moving was tough, especially when I was doing it so slowly. I didn't know where the shooter was and didn't want to draw attention to myself by accidentally knocking something off my lower bookshelf while changing positions. Worse yet, I didn't want to knock over my chair. Even hitting it the wrong way could push it into the free floating desk top and cause the shooter to investigate the noise. So, I moved slow and easy. When I was done, I picked up the receiver again and resumed counting the shots I'd just heard. I also noted which direction and from what floor each noise was coming. It occurred to me that the shooter and police were considerate in not firing their weapons until after I completed my position shift.

After that last volley of gunfire, it was silent for what seemed like a long time. This was an even more uncomfortable feeling than hearing the gunfire. Hearing the shooting at least gave me an idea where the shooter was located. But my silence didn't last long. I felt the heavy footfalls of a man coming down the aisle of cubicles behind me. It could be no other than the shooter. Where else would only one person be walking around? I whispered this to the 911 operator and told her that I was putting the phone's receiver down because I didn't want to give my position away. His footfalls stopped at the last cubicle directly behind mine. I prayed he would stay in that aisle, and wouldn't come over to mine. He stayed there for what seemed like an eternity, but in reality it may have been about ten to fifteen minutes. I could feel his footfalls stop as he just stood there, then I felt him move, first standing on one foot then on the other, then on both feet again. I felt his weight shift on those floors of ours. We could always tell when someone was walking down the aisles because the flooring was built such that when one walked on them, the footfalls are easily felt by those who are sitting in their cubicles. This was no different. I felt this person walking toward my cubicle, and his footfalls stopped behind me. He stayed on both feet and moved only barely for the next several minutes. Then he stepped to one side, and the next, with a pause for moments before shifting his weight as he moved.

At that point, I was sure he'd heard me breathing. I didn't move, I barely breathed. Even with the alarms blaring and the announcements replaying every few mintues, I dared not make a sound. Even with the gunpowder still hanging thick in the air like a curtain, threatening to make me cough, I struggled to maintain composure and dared not make a sound. He moved again, I remained frozen; my heartbeat was throbbing in my ears so loud I was sure he could hear it too. He moved a little more, I didn't move. He moved a step one way; I don't know which way but I didn't move. He stood there in that latest position for a few more minutes. Still I didn't move. He moved back where he was when he first came into the cubicle. I didn't move. He moved further into the cubicle and closer to me. I didn't move. He remained there. I didn't move although I really wanted to. I didn't even grab the phone. Now, I thought for sure that he could hear my heart beating, it was beating so hard. Then he moved away again toward the middle of the cubicle right behind me and stood there for a while. I didn't move. My mind was telling me the shooter knew someone was nearby but, wasn't quite sure where. It was as if he was listening for someone, and he was also trying to hide and plan his next steps.

Finally, he strolled off, his footfalls having an easy gait to them; no panic and no rush. I took a long slow silent breath and picked up the phone, but didn't talk yet, fearful that he was still too close and would hear me talk. After a few minutes, I spoke. "That was him and he was in the cubicle right behind me." I swear he knew I was here and was waiting for me to make any kind of sound so he could find out where I was. All I can think of is that Nina was in here and left so as to make it look like there was no one here. The sweat was dripping down my forehead and down my back; I was just now feeling it.

I wished the police were nearby so they could have caught him right then and there. I wished it was over. I wished so many things. I wished this secure building was really secure. I wished we had our cell phones so we could call each other to ensure we were all alive. Having them locked in lockboxes at the front doors to the building or left in our cars turned out to be of no help to us. We wouldn't have remembered to drag our cell phones with us anyway, but the safety of having them near us would have helped. I so much wanted to call my family! For now there was just an uneasy silence. The irony of ensuring our cell phones couldn't make it into the building, but weapons were allowed to slip through security was not lost on me.

After a pause, the 911 operator tells me the shooter is still loose and instructs me to stay put because they lost him and don't know where he may be headed. Her words are interrupted by yelling and the sound of people scattering in all directions. Now, the silence is very disconcerting; keeping me in suspense. My entire body is tense, not wanting to relax for fear of making a sound. After this long silence I suddenly hear, "Up there, he's up there!" I can hear the rush of boots on the flooring. There is no shooting, and no more sound of boots running; only silence follows. I surmised the police lost him again.

I counted the shots: one, two, three, four, five. Five shots and then another. Is that return fire? Then another set: one, two, three, four. Four shots accompanied by indistinguishable yelling. Another shot, more yelling, and then silence. I asked the operator if they got the shooter. Several minutes go by and then she says they didn't get him yet. Several more minutes go by. And then I hear more yelling followed by a shot; then another shot. It sounds like the shots came from the same gun. The next volley sounded like return fire from several different weapons. Silence. Moments pass, but they seem like hours. Then another shot. It sounds like return fire. This time I can't tell if it's from the shooter or the police. There is no yelling. No talking. No orders being given. Just that one shot and silence. I asked the 911 operator again if they got the shooter. A long pause from the operator. Then her response, "No, stay where you are!"

No more gunfire. Moments go by; again they seemed like hours. The silence from the lack of gunfire was almost deafening. Only the blare of that blasted fire alarm permiated the silence. It kept whaling in the silence along with the intercom that kept repeating, "Exit the building immediately," which was interspersed with the warning, "Shelter in place." How stupid that sounded. Confusing and contradictory at the same time. It was so ludicrous that I couldn't help thinking it must be a ploy used by the police to distract the shooter, and maybe mask the police movements.

I snapped out of it when I heard gunfire again. It sounded like the shots came from near the stairwell or the elevators; somewhere behind glass or in a conference room or office. Again, more silence. This time the shots were different. I could swear I'm now hearing a shotgun and a pistol. Did the shooter get his hands on a pistol? How could that happen? Do we now have a two handed shooter? Or are there two shooters? What kind of mad-man do we have here who knows how to simultaneously handle two guns?

More time goes by. A distant shot rings out. This time it sounds like it came from the third deck. Then another shot followed by return fire. Same gun type for both the initial shot and return fire. No yelling, no orders to surrender, no sound of tramping feet running away in haste. Again, I asked the 911 operator if they got him, but I already know the answer.

From where I'm sitting, the situation is so frustrating. The alarm competes with the intercom telling us to exit the building and another announcement that tells us to shelter in place. More silence, except for that blasted fire alarm; then more silence. By silence I mean the lack of gunfire. No gunfire and more long spells without the sound of gunfire. This guy obviously knows his way around the building.[4]

My mind drifts. It just occurred to me that this violence coupled with the shooter's knowledge of his weapon, the explicit familiarity

---

[4] Surveillance video released by the FBI on Wednesday (two days later) shows Alexis crouching around a corner on the fourth floor and walking briskly down a flight of stairs. The video shows the wall on the third deck that has Team Ship's bulletin board displaying their news. This could likely have been after he stayed in the cubicle area behind me for that period of time possibly thinking of where he should go next. The stairs down to the third deck are right around the corner from our area.

with the many hiding places and advantage points from which to shoot, as well as the ease with which he moves around causes me to wonder if he is an ex-employee that I fired from his job here at the Navy Yard. Had the shooter come back to extract revenge on me or someone else?

This thought is now vividly entrenched in the back of my mind. I just can't get it out of my head. The skill the shooter is adeptly displaying gives me reason to believe it is one of my former employees. The one with the violent tendencies, the one I just recently fired. Now I was really scared. If this was him, then he most definitely must be looking for me! Now I can only think back to the argument I had with him. He constantly interrupted me with a loud voice and said I was wasting his time. I remember him gathering his papers in a wrinkled mess and stomping out of my cubicle in frustration when I answered his questions calmly. Back then, he had violent tendencies to the point I had a security alarm system installed in my house to allay my fear of his coming to my house to shoot me after another incident at work between us.

I reasoned that because of his time in the service, he would know how to handle a weapon, many kinds of weapons, in fact. Having spent almost a year on the job on the fourth floor, he would have learned his way around all the nooks and crannies of the offices and cubicles. My mind was running wild because I didn't see the actual shooter. I only felt his footfalls and they felt heavy enough to have been my ex-employee's. Now I was really terrified. Could this ex-employee be that violent and have waited this long to come back and shoot up the place? If so, why didn't he come right to my cubicle and shoot me?

I recall that when I did let this employee go, it was done with dignity and I gave him every chance to leave with the respect he deserved as a wounded warrior, even if he couldn't do his job after all the training sessions that were spent with him. Okay, I am beginning to feel a little more at ease. Thinking back now, maybe that's why he didn't come directly after me. Maybe that's why he was waiting in the cubicle behind mine. Maybe he was waiting for my teleworking employee to show up. She was the one who trained him in his job and the person I appointed to help him when he needed it because she is the person who knew more about his job than I did. Could it be he was looking for this individual? Could that be why he shot out the cubicle window on what was once his own cubicle area when shooting at Nina? Was that the statement he was attempting to make?

The sound of gunfire snaps me back to the present. A single shot, but in the distance this time, too hard to tell the direction from where the shot came. There were no return shots. Where could this shot have been fired from? It didn't sound like it came from this floor. It sounded like it must have originated on the other side of the offices in the middle section of the building. This is the "Orange" Section that I used to find my area when I began working here. The building is so big; I had to find a method of identifying where my cubicle was. The three sections of the building were south to north, blue, orange, and purple, with the orange section housing the leaders of the IT section on the south of the west side of the building and the acquisition quality control and training on the north side. The shooter had already been there once. He couldn't have gone back there again, could he? Just then I hear a voice saying something unintelligible and then the name "Harris." I asked the 911 operator if there is a policeman by the name of Harris in the building. She didn't answer. I explained what I just heard, and told her if there wasn't a policeman by the name of Harris then there must be a partner the shooter was talking to. Then I hear the 911 operator begin to relay my message to an officer who must have been standing next to her. She says nothing to me.

After I heard the name, the shooter must have gone to the other side of the atrium. He must be in the Purple Section, as his interest was focused on the center and north sections of the building. The south side of the building held leadership and legal offices; and I felt those two sections would be well enough guarded that he might be unsuccessful at finding people to shoot there. I suspect he may have felt that way also. The Purple Section is furthest away from the river-side of the building where the majority of SEA04, the Logistics, Maintenance, and Operations offices are located. The police must be nowhere near him or they would have seen him, or at least heard him and followed the sound, eventually catching sight of him again. Silence again. Where could he be now? He's being careful because he's not shooting as much as he was earlier. The airborne gunpowder dust from the previous shots still hangs in the air; the stench wafting in my nose is chokingly repugnant. It doesn't want to follow the rules of gravity and settle to the floor. I would have thought it would dissipate after a while, but it doesn't. That grim reminder of where he was just minutes earlier still lingers in the air and my mind. No footfalls anywhere, not by the police, not by the shooter. Where was everyone?

Oh God! He's coming back. I hear his footsteps more than feel them. Now I feel them. I wondered why he didn't come down my cubicle aisle before and now I'm going to find out. Should I move to the cubicle opening so I can grab his weapon away from him as he walks by? That may be the only chance I have to survive, even if it is only a slim one. If I move this chair now he'll know I'm here because he'll hear the sound and will more than likely jump at me with his gun blazing. But suddenly, I realize it's too late to do anything. I can literally feel him coming down the aisle to my doorway. I'm as good as dead! I have no chance. This is it. As long as I'm going to die, I might as well pull my bag out of the way and get ready to push the chair at him. I can use this phone handle as some protection to keep my head from taking a direct shot.

Before I can take any action I see the barrel of his gun. It's coming slowly past the edge of my cubicle wall. I'm ducking as tightly into the corner recesses under my desk as possible, hoping, praying he doesn't see me. Sweat is running down my back. My heart is pounding so hard I can feel it pulsing in my neck. Wait! It's not a shotgun, it's a pistol! Why would he be weilding a pistol instead of his rifle? Where is his shotgun? Did he use up all his ammo and have to ditch his shotgun, leaving him with the pistol I heard him use in answer to the police earlier? This doesn't make sense. As the gun moves forward I can see two hands holding the pistol. That's not a normal stance for a killer. Then a body comes into view. I'm ready to push my chair out at him and throw my bag at him, followed closely by my shoes. I'm prepared and in a stance, holding the receiver in my hand, and still crouched under my desk. I see a bright green vest. A bright green vest? A cop? What the hell? The 911 operator didn't say they got the shooter, so what's a police officer doing here looking for me instead of the shooter?

He points his pistol directly at me.

CHAPTER 4

The Evacuation

"Show me your hands!" commanded the cop in a stern and fierce voice. I held up my hands just over the seat of my webbed chair, one still holding the receiver with the 911 operator on the other end. More sternly, and in a louder voice, he said, "I said, show me your hands!!!" I held my hands up and waived them, including the hand still holding the telephone receiver. He was looking at me mostly through my webbed chair, and my hands entirely through my webbed chair. My phone receiver was black, as was my webbed chair, but you could still see through that chair and under it too, for that matter. I was thinking that it was the bright pink jacket that gave me away. Certainly, nothing says, "Hey look at me!" like the outfit I was wearing.

Perhaps he was satisfied that I showed him my hands. His next command was, "Come out of there with your hands up." His pistol was still pointed at me; dead center. After the dreadful ordeal I just went through, now I was being treated like a criminal! I realize the cop had to be sure I wasn't a shooter, but to now have a policeman holding a gun right in my face was extremely disconcerting. The operator told me several times not to leave my hiding place until a policeman came to get me because he would safely escort me out of the building. This had to be the person who was going to escort me out of the building, but it didn't feel good to have his gun in my face as an indication he was there to help me.

I told the 911 operator the police were here and that I had to hang up now. She said that was okay. I thanked her and hung up, feeling like I was losing my only link to the outside world; my only friend in the world. I was so sad to lose my link with the outside, and with sanity, as I hung up that receiver; a lump formed in my throat as I crawled out of my hiding place and hung up the phone. Since my first introduction to the policeman was his pointing a gun in my face, I wasn't inclined to look at him as a rescuer. Once I crawled out of my dark little hiding spot, the policeman's manner changed. He said he was going to get me out of here. The hiding space under my desk, with my lifeline to the outside, the 911 operator, was a part of my life for nearly an hour. Now I was facing uncertainty with this strange new person, a policeman wearing a vest identifying him as such, and carrying a mere pistol against a shooter whose location was unknown, and with who-knows how many weapons now. How did I know I could trust this policeman? After all, I hadn't been on the phone with him for most of the last hour. I only just met him, and not in the nicest of ways either. It didn't seem like I had a choice though.

There were no feelings of elation, and no smiles coming from me as I was putting on my walking sandals. I put my wedge sandals back on instead of my heels. Somehow, I figured I was going to be doing a lot of walking and heels just wouldn't cut it. The sandals were what I preferred to have on when I headed for a walk, especially long walks. A last minute impulse made me reach over and disconnect my laptop. I literally pushed the release button and popped it out of its docking station—CAC and all. When the policeman heard the pop, he turned and scolded me, saying, "There's nothing here worth dying for." As I snatched my bag from the floor in my other hand, I was going to snipe back at him that he didn't know my senior supervisor, but thought better of it. Besides, by then I was already behind him laptop and bag in hand, and wearing sandels ready to follow.

On the way to the exit, the cop held his pistol out in front of him. He walked forward in a semi crouching position toward Nina's desk with me in trail. Since he was walking like that, I thought I'd better walk like that too. It must have looked silly with the two of us walking in a semi-crouched position in single file. When we approached Nina's cubicle, I was shocked at the shattered glass in the front cubicle across from her desk, but ecstatic that there was no blood in her cubicle. I didn't see her, or her body, and to me that meant there was a possibility she had actually gotten away and was alive.

As we walked past Russ' area, I noticed a green shotgun shell lying on the floor. There wasn't blood in the area so I knew Russ wasn't the recipient of that shot. I couldn't see all the way back inside Kammie's cubicle so couldn't discern how she fared during the shooting spree. There were only 5 shots executed in our immediate area, the one by the banister, the two back toward the IT section, the one aimed at Nina that broke the glass in the cubicle across from her, and another one somewhere near the back hallway near the offices, but still in our section. The only shot that obviously hit an object was the one that hit the glass of the cubicle. When the policeman escorted me out, he led me in the direction past the atrium so I didn't get a chance to look through the kitchen area toward the IT section. When we headed toward the North stairwell, I didn't look back toward the hallway so I didn't see if there were any shells on the floor. It surprised me that I didn't see the shells from the shot at the end of our row; the one from Nina and the empty cubicle's window. This makes sense because though the shooting began on our floor near my area, most of the shots I heard and was reporting locations to the operator on were in different areas of the building so the shells would be in those places. I think the officer was walking fast in order to keep me from taking a good look around on the way to the stairway.

The contents of that empty shell casing had to have been used to pepper something somewhere and I was trying to figure out where. Going by the sounds of the first shots, this was the area where the shooter was headed to after being focused, or focused on after beginning in the IT section. To me, it would be reasonable to believe the shell was ejected by the shooter when he turned to walk away from the atrium banister in the process of cocking his shotgun preparing for his next shot, because he never went back down that aisle. It was two-thirds of the way down the aisle toward his decision point for his next turn. That is a long time to wait to cock his shotgun for the next shot, even if it was the first of what would be many volleys. Was it a moment of forgetfulness? Linear thinking? Processing the next steps while forgetting to think about getting the next round into the chamber? We'll never know.

Other than the alarm, to which I was now acclimated, there was deadly silence around. No one was walking or talking, not even running, and certainly not screaming. I heard no footfalls except our own. I felt I could have dropped a pin over the balcony and, except for the incessant fire alarm and loudspeaker, was sure I could hear it hit the floor of the atrium. That's how quiet it was now. There was no din of activity, and not even the yelling of officers from one to the other. It was almost as if they gave up and were going to wait for the shooter to give himself up.

As I followed the officer, he didn't lead me to the nearest stairwell. He skipped past the open atrium and quietly slipped to the stairwell closer to the purple section across from the open atrium area. As we approached the vast openness of the atrium, I wasn't sure I wanted to pass that entire expanse. Even though we were on the fourth floor, not knowing where the shooter was made me very hesitant to expose myself to the wide openness, a blatently easy target for the shooter. The feeling I had was indescribable. It invoked intense fear, anxiety, angst and undescribable emotions ranging from distrust to desire to run in the opposite direction from this person taking me in what I knew was the wrong direction, the person I just met; making me wonder why I was letting him take me into harm's way. I just couldn't understand why he was taking me through that danger all over again.

The stairwell leading outside the building and to safety was just 10 feet around the corner to the left, yet the policeman took me forty feet past an open atrium and 10 more feet to the stairwell in the purple section. I wouldn't know until much later why. I felt I was in harm's way when he took me all that distance rather than just around the corner. You better believe I walked low and as stealthily as I could while following him, knowing he was leading me past an open atrium and my possible death. When we got to the stairwell, he opened the door, yelled, "Code blue, code blue, one coming down." He then told me to go all the way to the bottom without stopping and to go out the door on the outside ground floor. He said someone would be there to meet me.

When I got to the bottom and opened the door to the outside I stood on the steps and breathed fresh air for the first time since the shooting began. No gunpowder drifting in my nostrils and no pallor of gunfire smoke hanging thick in the air. Then, seeing no one, I started to head toward the river side of the building to our pre-arranged meeting place. We were trained to head toward the water side of the building and meet at the flagpole in the park during our fire drills. That is where I was headed because I saw no one. In reaction to all my fire drill training, I started down the steps from the landing area and headed toward the flagpole.

Just as I reached the bottom step a voice behind me cried out, "Hey, you!" I turned around, and sure enough, there was someone to meet me. He just wasn't where I expected him to be. He told me to walk over to him. Then he told me to walk down the walkway to the next police officer and stay next to the wall because they thought the shooter was on the roof. I hugged the wall on the way down the side of that building. There were police or SWAT lining the side of the building all the way to the street and every 12 feet or so I'd stop and then head to the next officer. When I got to the street the officer there pointed me to cross the street. He told me to run as fast as I could so I wouldn't be targeted by the shooter. I ran to the side of the next building. The officer across the street encouraged me to keep running to the end of that building to avoid becoming a target while attempting to escape.

I was directed across the street, then told to walk along the side of the parking garage situated across the street from Building 197, and up the steps to the officer next to the building at the top of the hill. Those steps felt to me like I was climbing stairs to heaven. They kept going and going and going, up and up and up. If I wasn't really winded by the time I arrived at the steps, I was definitely winded by the time I was halfway up the climb. By the time I got to the top of the steps I could have used a chair to sit in and a little time to rest. Going up the steps in Building 197 is hard to do and there are very handy banisters to help me. There are two flights of stairs between each floor with a double-height banister on each flight of stairs in Building 197, so I can help pull myself to the next step. This stairway had a simple banister that I heavily relied on all the way up only stopping briefly for a little bit of a rest midway up. When I got to the top there was an officer who directed me as to which way to go next.

The officer told me to turn right and cross a ten foot walk and then take another right turn and head down the street almost parallel to the same steps I just came up. By now I wasn't the slightest bit interested in walking, much less running anywhere. Again I was encouraged to run so I wasn't a target for the shooter. This I did until I was sure there was a building between me and Building 197. There were numerous officers posted along the route and now they had me veer off to the left away from Building 197. Although they were still encouraging me to run, I was so exhausted that I turned to one of them and told him I just couldn't run anymore. Knowing I was safely out of sight of the building's roof, I just continued to walk because by now I was totally out of breath.

There were officers posted about every 15 to 20 feet along the entire evacuation route, from the first "Hey you," officer, to the last "Go to that doorway in that building," officer. They told me to walk over to the clinic. However, as I neared the clinic, the officer on the corner of the clinic building pointed me left to another building and told me to go to the doorway on the side of the building across the street from the clinic instead.

This building was fairly large and while there were people lined around the desk to put their names on muster lists, I walked past that desk and went down the hallway to see if I could find anyone from our department. I found no one. Then someone told me there were people on the fifth floor. So, I continued to the fifth floor to find someone, anyone from my department. After looking around the fifth floor hallway and the conference room I still didn't find anyone from our office. When I didn't find them on the fifth floor, I returned to the first floor and got in line to sign in on the muster list I'd passed up earlier.

I needed to find out if there were other places where people may have gone. I found Captain Theodore, who was in charge of this building, and explained to him that I was trying to locate anyone from my office to see if they got out and were mustered somewhere else. I had a supervisor and employees for whom I had to determine status. I knew my supervisor would be looking for a report on my people. I gave Captain Theodore a list of names and he went to check with the other buildings where people were mustering. He returned to me with the news that none of my names were on any of the muster lists he checked.

Just then an announcement was being made that the conference room on the fifth floor was being set up with a news feed about the day's events. So, back up to the fifth floor I went to watch the news feed. The anteroom to the conference room on the fifth floor of this building was set up with a lounge-type layout. There were overstuffed chairs in one corner with telephones on two sides of a row of chairs. There were tables set up with computers in the other corner of the room that could act as workstations if necessary. There were also chairs brought in and set up in small circles in the remaining space. I sat in the fifth floor side-conference ante-room and began making telephone calls. It was important for me to try locating employees in my department to find out if they were safe, and let them know I had also gotten out safely. I had some important numbers written down for reference and needed to find that little sheet now. I needed more numbers than were on my reference sheet and hoped I could get them from someone I would be calling.

As I was looking through my bag for a writing implement, I found I'd forgotten to take out my cell phone when I left my car in the commuter lot and it was in the very bottom of my bag, now available to me. Some of those numbers I needed were in my cell phone contacts. My teleworking employee tried to contact me during the shooting but I was otherwise engaged with the 911 operator. I texted my teleworking employee with my cell phone first to let her know I got out and was looking for the others. We texted back and forth for about 20 minutes, but my battery was quickly dying so I had to get off the phone. I dug in the bottom of my bag to find something to write on so I could get the phone numbers I needed before the battery died on my phone. The only thing I could find to write on was a crumpled napkin that was under my wallet, umbrella, thermos and everything else, except the kitchen sink. It had been there long enough to become wrinkled, and certainly unappealing for use as a napkin. However, in desperate straights, I managed to get my pen to write well enough on it to be readable at the moment so I could dial using the phone near my seat in attempts to find my co-worker, employee and boss. I used what little battery life I had to write down the important numbers I had stored in my cell phone. The kids, my boss, all my employees, even the teleworkers' numbers were needed. I went through my entire address book to make sure I had everyone's telephone number.

After I texted my teleworker, she called my supervisor's teleworking employee to let her know the situation. I then thought it might be a good idea to let my husband know I was all right in case he had heard the news and was worried. So, I gave him a call. It went straight to his voicemail and I left a message. Then I called my daughter to let her know what was going on and to let her know I couldn't find my employees. She offered to let her siblings know my situation. I gratefully accepted her offer because I knew looking for the people I needed to find would occupy most of my time.

I went through my entire address book in my cell phone to make sure I had written down everyone's telephone number I might need. I had my supervisor's mobile and home phone numbers stored, but they were put in with such haste, I couldn't immediately identify which one was the home number and which one was the mobile number. Right now, there wasn't any easy way to make these changes on my basic model phone, but it needed to be done; just not now. So changing the numbers to identify which was the home and which was the cell number would wait, once again, until there was time.

I was thinking how funny it was to get focused on small things that didn't matter in stressful situations. Anyway, the thought occurred to me that my supervisor would have left her cell phone in her car like many folks who work on the Navy Yard and drive in to work, do.

Therefore, I thought it might not be that easy for me to contact her. When I had all the numbers written down, I felt better because I had access to a regular telephone.

I called my teleworking employee to give her my current contact number. We discussed some of the work that was in progress and the way ahead for other work. Then we had to get off the phone so I could continue looking for the rest of our group.

CHAPTER 5

Where are they?

"Hello, Laurel."

I recognized the voice as I answered the land line phone next to me while sitting in the overstuffed chair outside the conference room we'd evacuated to. It was one of our teleworkers calling me. She said, "There's still a group of our people who were herded into one of the rooms in Building 197." They were shoved into one of our training rooms with a bunch of other people to get them out of the hallways and out of danger while looking for the second shooter. The individuals in that group were taking turns using a single blackberry to make calls. They were letting others know where they were and that they were okay. I found out that our supervisor and another co-worker of mine were both in that group. This was a great relief. I now knew where two members of our office were. The only problem was they were still in the building with a possible second shooter. Though the policemen told me the shooter was on the roof, it didn't mean he would stay there, and they believed there was a second shooter that was not yet identified.

After finding out where the group was hiding, I called the 911 operator back to let her know there was still a group of workers locked in the training room that needed to be rescued. The operator asked how many were in the group and where the training room was located. Of course the teleworker didn't think about getting that information from anyone in the group; she was just ecstatic that some of our office survived and were in a semi-safe place when she called me with the information. I explained to the 911 operator that there were two training rooms in the front hallway across from the cafeteria and two training rooms in the back hallway across from the cafeteria. I told the operator that each training room had two entrance doors. They would be the first two rooms encountered when one entered each of these hallways. I further explained there was the possibility that classes were in session and, if so, those individuals would need to be rescued also. I didn't know if classes were going on at the time, but I emphasized that each training room needed to be checked.

After making the 911 operator aware of the need to rescue people in the training rooms, I continued my search for Nina. Since I didn't see any blood in or near her cubicle, I was now running on the assumption that she may have escaped harm and was waiting in one of the muster areas. I just couldn't find her, even after two hours of looking everywhere I could and calling everyone I knew. I finally went to Captain Theodore and had Nina officially declared missing. I was now not in the best of shape. I felt sure I'd lost a very good friend, not to mention the best employee I had.

I called my husband back because I wanted the comfort of hearing his voice, of knowing he was there, and the knowledge that I would see him again sometime in my future. Instead of voicemail this time, I actually got ahold of him. I asked him if he listened to the voicemail I left earlier when I called. He didn't. He'd just gotten in from getting the tractor pulled out of the pond where it had gotten mired. I had to smile at that. It is a typical fiasco in a day of our lives. I told him about the shooting and that I would be home late. He asked if he could come up and get me, but we were finding out from the news that the base was closed and no one was allowed on or off the base; even walking off-base wasn't permitted. Since we were on the "community" phone, I couldn't talk long. We briefly ran through different possibilities for getting me home. Then I told him I'd call later when I found out what was going to happen to us next so we could execute one of our plans to get me home. He later told me that he was glued to the TV after our conversation.

There were two of us who stationed ourselves near one of the several phones made available to us. I made some initial phone calls to key people, then the other individual made some calls. When calls came in, one of us would answer the phone and yell out the name of the person who was wanted. Someone would go about looking for that person. There was one person who came over to make a call, and from his demeanor, looked like he planned on talking for a while. I let him know, and probably rather rudely, that the phone was for emergency incoming and outgoing calls and was not to be tied up for too long with superfluous chit-chat. He got the message and hung up shortly. Later, a call came in for him, we paged him, and someone went about yelling out his name. He came to the phone and talked, but only for a short time. Then he hung up letting the phone remain available for others to use. He got the message that the phone was a community phone and not to be tied up for long periods of time.

As I sat in that chair, when I wasn't making the occasional phone call or receiving incoming calls, I was continuing on with the work I needed to finish. I thought it would be a good idea to make use of the time I was spending waiting for the base to open and our eventual release, to finish the work I needed to do. One man sat on the arm of my overstuffed chair to make a call to his wife and explained how his boss cracked his office door open after the shooter passed, and motioned him to come quickly into the safety of his office, saving his life. Another conversation I overheard was a woman desperately trying to get in touch with her husband. She tried her home number and his cell number, but both attempts went to voicemail. She was on the verge of tears knowing he was not aware of whether she was alive or not. For over an hour she kept trying to connect with her husband. When she finally reached him, she burst out in tears. Many people called home simply to let their spouses know what happened and they would be late coming home. Others had to call home to make arrangments to have children picked up and provide suggestions for dinner. Needless to say, the phone was almost continuously in use.

Another one of our teleworkers called me on the land line to let me know Nina made it out and was at the NAVFAC (Naval Facilities) building. I cried. She went on to tell me that Nina had run back out toward Russ's area and Russ grabbed her hand and they both went down the middle staircase in the back of the building. This was the same stairway I couldn't figure out why we didn't use when the policeman came to get me. She told her friends at NAVFAC to make sure they called around to let me know she was OK, because she had to let her supervisor know where she was. That may have been them calling me on the phone while I was talking to the 911 operator. I'll never know.

As far as I know, NAVFAC never did merge their muster list with those of the other muster groups, or even with any of the lists that would eventually be merged with those of the other buildings. I'll never figure out why they missed the opportunity of sharing the lists amongst muster locations. Surely there should have been a central operations collecting names and searching for missing individuals who were reported being in the building. I know that as a supervisor, it certainly would have saved me a lot of heartache and time trying to account for my employees and other coworkers.

When I got off the phone, I went right downstairs to the front desk and asked for the person in charge of muster lists. I told him to take

Nina off the list of missing people, and that I'd found her. I also told him she was at NAVFAC and was safe. When I turned to leave I was in tears. The Captain happened to be walking in my direction as I was headed back. He looked at me sadly and asked what was wrong. I told him I found my employee and these were tears of Joy. He smiled and squeezed my arm, knowingly.

I found that the police rescued Wilma and Jill, along with others from that group in the classroom, and herded them toward the clinic the same way I was herded in that same direction earlier. Since they'd had such a hard time of the ordeal with Jill being faced by the shooter, locked in an office for an undetermined amount of time, then herded into the classroom for hours until I found where they were and called 911 to have them rescued, they were sent to the clinic to be tended-to. I found out much later that our resident NCIS agent was downstairs pushing people together and herding them into rooms to get them out of harm's way. He had herded them into the training room to keep them safe.

Once in another building on the base, no one was allowed out of that building to move to another building. That was your home away from home until such time as the FBI told your building owner you were allowed to gather in the street to walk to the Conference Center. This is where we were to be interviewed by the FBI then placed on buses to be driven to the National's Stadium. So even though Wilma and Jill were only in the building across the street from me, neither one of us was allowed to move to be with the others or vice versa.

The National's baseball team had a game scheduled for the evening of September 16th. After the shooting at the Navy Yard, the National's canceled their game out of respect for the victims of the shooting. Because of the fact that there was no game being held at the National's Stadium now, they offered it to the Navy Yard as a muster point that could be sequestered from the news agencies, closely guarded and that was away from the Navy Yard, and out of the public eye to allow the survivors a chance to recover, seek counseling, where needed, and arrange for transportation home or to their commuter lots and then home, if chosen. I had to wonder how many people chose to leave their vehicles in the commuter lots and have a family member come pick them up at the stadium? The layout of the stadium entranceway was on a street that could be cordoned off from other means of access and met the needs of being secure and private for those affected by the shooting.

I mentioned earlier that I called my daughter to let her know what had happened and that I was safe. After I called her, she proceeded to call her three brothers to catch them up on my status. I didn't know it at the time, but all of the boys tried to call me on my cell phone but my battery was almost dead so I had already turned it off. However, by the next day, they were all calling me because I hadn't answered my voicemail.

CHAPTER 6

The Heroes

The lady sitting on the other side of the telephone table said she saw the shooter shoot a co-worker. That got me thinking; how does someone see their co-worker shot and be able to sit there so calmly only hours afterward? Of course, I had the shooter standing in the cubicle behind mine for several minutes and here I sit. Somehow, my ordeal suddenly pales in comparison to this woman's tribulation.

Now that I knew my own coworkers were accounted for, I thought I'd get to know the lady sitting on the other side of the table. She was sitting there in her seat, with her hands folded over her stomach manning the phone, sometimes using the phone, and sometimes talking to her friends who walked up to her for a short conversation. We'd been sitting next to each other for most of the time we'd been sequestered in this building, nearly three hours already. Most of the women were talking in small groups. They apparently knew each other from their workplaces in building 197. I wasn't sure how to engage in conversation with any of them. They were all perfect strangers to me and I didn't belong to any of their small groups. However, I did manage to introduce myself to the lady sitting across from me.

This lady told me she was in the cafeteria when they heard a loud noise. Out of curiosity, she explained, a gentleman in the cafeteria opened the door and looked out into the hallway to see what the noise was. What she saw stunned her. He was instantly shot in the head. She relayed this information casually, as if she were talking about something that happens everyday. I couldn't believe she was acting so casually about such an awful incident! There were no tears, no tension in her voice, no anxiety about what happened, just no sign that she was upset about that shooting. From my experience, I know that the distance from the back corner of the fourth floor across the atrium to the side door of the cafeteria is only a little over 50 feet. There was no way with a shotgun someone could miss the gentleman from that short range. She acted as if nothing out of the ordinary had happened in her day except that she was made to sit in a building other than her own with nothing to do but wait. She didn't display signs of irritation, until later in the day as the hours wore on without sign of our dismissal. Somehow, my ordeal suddenly pales in comparison to this woman's tribulation. Yet, of her few phone calls, her directions were to get dinner ready because she wasn't sure when we would be released.

The situation got me to thinking about literally being in the wrong place at the wrong time. If the man hadn't been in the cafeteria at that particular moment, if he hadn't heard the noise, or if he hadn't poked his head out to investigate, he most likely would still be with us today. He wouldn't have been shot—just like that, his life ended! His simple curiosity caused him to open the door and to peek out into the atrium. Then again, no one expects to be fired upon in a secure government building, on a closed Navy base, when it's just another day at the office.

He probably got up in the morning, said good-bye to the wife and kids, promised the wife he'd help with homework, or housework, or repairs to something around the house that night when he got home; probably even planned to leave a little early just so he could get a head start on whatever it was he needed to get done. Without giving it a second thought, he left his house that morning expecting to return in the evening just like every other day. Like me, he had a thousand items he had to get done and just like that—BANG! His life ended in a flash and the world changed for his family. My thoughts were that here was a person who was minding his own business and decided to investigate an unusual sound—not regularly heard in the building—to see what it was and to see if someone needed help. I'm sure he was just trying to identify the source of the noise and determine what was going on. There was no expectation of a weapon being the cause of the noise, yet that is what ended his life and changed everything for his family. I'm wondering if his family even knows what has happened to him. Like my family, they are probably going about their busy lives right now oblivious to the tragic events that will unfold for them sometime later on today. So heartbreaking to think about.

While I was moving back and forth trying to find a place to sit so others could use the seat next to the phone, I happened to sit next to a man who was talking to his wife on his cell phone. He was explaining to her what happened in his office this morning. I overheard his side of a phone conversation about an employee who was shot in the head. When he got off the phone, I admitted to him that I was eavesdropping and asked about the employee. He said the shooter just aimed his weapon at the man and shot him in the head at which point a woman in the cubicle across from him ran over to stem the bleeding. Apparently, she had been a corpsman in the Navy and knew what to do in this situation. Even in the face of all the danger, this courageous woman ran to help her co-worker. The man explained that after the shooter moved on, the woman got help and dragged the shooting victim out to the elevators and then the front door where they could get him to the ambulance that was called for them. I was told she even accompanied him to the hospital. The co-worker I was talking to also dialed 911, but when his supervisor opened the door to his office and summoned him in, he hung up the phone and ran into the office to take cover.

I also learned that a finance Captain was escorting a group of people out the 5th floor stairwell and down past the 4th floor on the way to the first floor. It seems the shooter saw the group, opened the stairwell door and shot into the pack, hitting one of the women in the shoulder. At that point, the Captain urged the group back up to the 5th floor and out on to the roof. When they reached the roof, a helicopter crew spotted them and the wounded woman. They hovered over as close as they could maneuver and picked her up. The helicopter crew then medivaced her to a local hospital. Since the site was an active hostile site, the helicopter flew off without taking the stretcher inside the cabin. When it landed, calls went out for a gurney and wheelchair, whichever came first. I found out that the wounded woman said, "The heck with this, I'm getting out of here." She got out of the stretcher and walked into the hospital on her own.

I heard of another person who was a member of the facilities team, but was seated with the IT group. His job was to situate with that group and use the location as a centralized site from which to work. Apparently, this allowed him to fan out to locations where he was assigned repair tasks by the facilities department. It turns out this man saw the shooter coming and apparently figured if he was going to get shot, he might as well get shot fighting back. With the budget cutbacks over the past several years, the cubicles we have are old and falling apart. For the most part, they can't be solidly screwed together. One would be more accurate in saying they aren't held together, they lean together. (I've knocked a cubicle wall off just by leaning against it). This facility guy's strategy was to grab the side of his cubicle and throw it at the shooter. He thought it would catch the shooter off guard. His bravery may have saved lives. It allowed people just enough time to get away while the shooter was preoccupied with a cubicle wall being thrown at him. Unfortunately, the shooter shot this brave man through the material of the cubicle wall, instantly killing him. This man is a hero in my book because, in the end, several people were able to escape because of his action.

The bravery displayed in these stories alone makes me proud to be among the NAVSEA family. These men and women are true heroes. From the corpsman whose training took over without a thought about her own safety in an attempt to save her co-worker's life, to the man who threw his cubicle wall at the shooter to stem the tirade in the hopes of giving his co-workers time to get away. Heroes, all of them!

There are lessons to be learned here in our sanctuary too. After I located my employee, Nina, the world seemed to slow down. This gave me time to sit back, talk to people, and to contemplate lessons learned. I learned to not be too nosy; it could get you killed. If you must investigate a situation, do it with caution; it could save your life. I also observed people approaching their newfound situation in different ways. I saw people who I knew were very impatient, display increased patience. I saw others start demonstrating impertinence. Still, there were others who just wanted to get out of here and go home so they could forget about what they heard or saw and move on to the next day. It was eye-opening to see how people adjusted to the situation in which they found themselves. People became cognizant of the needs of others to use the phone to call family and notify supervisors and co-workers of their status. I did not observe tempers flaring anywhere on any of the floors, even as the day stretched into evening. We'd all been through a horrific experience, some more than others. Although everyone responded differently, in the end everyone pitched in to help others. Our job, moving forward, is to move forward, use these lessons from today to remember and learn, fix the system, and focus on the true problem, not the problem du jour.

After we were out of Building 197 and in our evacuation buildings, there were people in these buildings who helped those who'd suffered trauma during the shooting. While enduring the experience of being shot at and the luck of moving just the right direction at just the right time to be missed by the projectiles, Nina escaped to NAVFAC where she felt safe. She worked there before being hired in our department almost a year ago and her friends there took care of her when she arrived, seeking help and shelter. As we were suddenly placed in strange buildings, the occupants of those buildings did everything they could to make us feel at home, even to the point of setting up phones for us so we could contact our family members to let them know we were all right. As the phone became a lifeline to the outside, family members began to call in to find out information about their loved ones. They knew how it felt to contact a voicemail and just leave a message; and what the person on the other side would think when hearing that message. They knew that person would want to talk to the person leaving the message, and helped by ensuring the person being called was able to talk to the caller. Talking to these people let me know there was a lot of caring in the group of people who'd found themselves in our building. Even knowing about this caring group didn't help me feel any better until I'd found my supervisor and employee though. When I'd found them, and knew they were safe, I was so relieved I felt like a great burden was lifted from my shoulders and my heart felt like it started beating again.

I'd found out about the heroes of our day, some of them anyway, and the price they paid. I found my heart in my throat every time I thought of what was going on in that building each time a single shot rang out. Even today my frustration goes up not just one notch, but several, when I think about the process or requirement behind the "stop, police, put your hands up," mentality that allowed the shooter to get away and more people in Building 197 to get shot. I wonder at what point someone got smart enough to think or to issue the order, to shoot first and ask questions later that finally brought that terrible shooter down. And I wonder why that couldn't have happened long before the time it did.

The shooter fit the bill of a coward; he could only face these people with a gun in hand, in an uneven fight because he knew that was the only way he could win. He could only shoot, and even did that from afar, or from behind, or above, and only when his prey was at a disadvantage. He would need a periscope to look up to a worm. But he couldn't win the power of caring these people had and still have for each other. So many brave people—so many heroes—so many who paid the ultimate price.

CHAPTER 7

The Sanctuary

"Stop, police, put your hands up!" BANG! Another victim goes down.

I find myself reliving this scene over and over again, asking at what point are the police going to get smart enough to issue an order to shoot first and ask questions later? My mind was wondering how many more people have to get shot before the police learn the shooter is not going to drop his weapon and just surrender to them. My frustration goes up several notches just thinking about the mentality that allows so many innocents to get shot. Please, someone issue an order to shoot first and ask questions later! So many brave people—so many heroes—many who paid the ultimate price. I snap back to reality.

Refugees from Building 197 were herded into many of the other buildings on the Navy Yard. These buildings became sanctuaries. It didn't matter whether it was a small building that could only hold 20 people or one large enough to hold hundreds; each sanctuary was hosted by someone who made us feel as welcome as possible. Every instance in which I found myself after exiting Building 197; I found we were treated with kindness and compassion. In the building where I finally ended my journey out of hell, Captain Theodore was in charge.

It was the first time I was able to let my guard down enough to gather my thoughts.

Throughout the morning, as more people came into the building, Captain Theodore opened more floors to us so the influx of people being evacuated could be accommodated without crowding on the first floor. This avoided over-crowding, and kept the majority of people from standing around on the first floor. We ended up spread out on only three floors; the first, second and fifth floors of the building. This building was the second largest building on the base, and could accommodate quite a large number of people, but only if the additional floors were made accessable. The fifth floor had a huge conference room outfitted with widescreen displays that were connected to a feed to FOX News. Earlier, the Captain had asked for the FOX News feed to be sent to the large displays so we could be aware of what the news was telling the outside world.

I think Captain Theodore understood what happened to our worlds today. Not only did he open up his building to us, but the entirety of the building's occupants managed to come up with food for us. Everything from oatmeal to chips and cookies to cases of soda magically appeared on the tables at the front of the room. This helped see us through the day. No one was allowed off base so no one could make "food runs." We all needed to make do with what was available. Near the end of the day a jar of peanut butter even showed up. I'm sure Captain Theodore just asked his people if they had refreshments available, and they brought out everything they could find. They did everything they could to make us comfortable.

The Captain made announcements of any information as he was made aware of it. Though we had a computer feed of Fox news on the flatscreens in the big conference room on the fifth floor, not everyone availed themselves of the news. The news on those screens managed to draw many people from each of the floors; enough to fill the huge conference room, and they were glued to the screen. They wanted to know what was going on and what the outside world was learning about the ongoing situation at the Navy Yard. The news, as seen from the outside, helped us understand what the public was seeing, and as we saw what the public was seeing, we wanted to know more about what was going on. After all, this had happened to us and to our workplaces, our friends, our workday. The events of the day disrupted our normal routines and they had occurred in what we thought was a secure building, causing our world to be turned upside down. When we correlated the news on TV with what we personally experienced this morning, it finally started to sink in that our workday routines and our concept of exactly what security meant were no longer valid. To me, this was mind-boggling.

Mid-morning the Captain came on the loudspeaker to let us know that the shooter had been killed by the police. At about this time Fox news was also reporting the death of the shooter. When the shooter's name appeared, a person standing at the lectern turned up the speaker so everyone could hear. Even those of us in the ante-conference side room heard the name. Hearing the name eased my mind about the shooter being an ex-employee. Soon the news agencies found a picture to display on the screen. I never saw the man's face. I only heard and felt his footsteps as he walked behind my cubicle and moved around, and heard his voice as he yelled his epithet and spoke to "Harris." The rest of the time I heard the shots from his gun and the return fire from the police. This was my first sight of the man. It was not a very unpleasant moment for me. I could only imagine what it was for Nina, if she was seeing the news on a screen where she was. The picture of this person will always be in my mind now. Even though I didn't encounter him like some of my co-workers did, he so disrupted my life, and caused so much distress to me that I find it hard to think I will ever forget him.

When I heard the shooter was no longer a threat, my mind reverted back to what I was doing when the shootings began. Oh yeah, I was on a tight deadline to get a project completed. It's funny I now find myself thinking about work that I had to do when I just came through a life-threatening experience. I'm not sure why, but I suddenly felt compelled to get back to work. After all, I still had my marching orders from last Friday and the deadline for finishing my work was close at hand. I'm not sure if it was the shock of what I just went through or whether I was suffering an emotional release from the tension that brought my attention back to what I was doing when the first shot rang out.

As I was thinking about the shooter, the Captain came on the loudspeaker to let us know they were still looking for another shooter. I found myself wondering if the other shooter's name was Harris, the name I heard the shooter call out during his shooting rampage; the one I asked the 911 operator to ask the police liaison about; explaining that if there wasn't a policeman having that name then there might be an accomplice. All throughout the morning the same news stories were repeated over and over again by the TV broadcasters. The cameras on the streets around the Navy Yard showed an empty M Street. All traffic was stopped; prohibited from going past the Navy Yard. As we looked out the windows of our sanctuary, we could only imagine all the news trucks with their cameras set up; newscasters chatting about anything and everything they could think of to keep viewer attention. We could see it on the screens. We also saw a very large number of police cars lining the streets.

I remember working on a policy letter throughout the morning, but needed to put some finishing touches on it. Once these minor edits were completed, it would finally be ready to hand over to a handful of people on the distribution list after approval of my supervisor. My plan was to forward the finished document to my supervisor the next time I had internet access. Since I had dragged my work laptop out of my cubicle when I was escorted out of Building 197, I opened the document and started working on it. There wasn't much editing to be done. Halfway through the editing process though, I got a low battery warning. I saved my work because I knew I was finished for the day until I could recharge the battery. So the document would have to wait for another day to be completed.

Again, the Captain came on the loudspeaker to inform us that until further notice, no one would be allowed to take their cars out of the garage. Not long afterward he came back on to tell us the Navy Yard was closed and no one would be allowed to leave unless they used one of the buses scheduled to leave from the conference center. We were under total lockdown and since no privately operated vehicles would be allowed to leave the base tonight, I became concerned about getting home. I didn't have a vehicle there, but rode in on a vanpool, which now wouldn't be leaving; so even though I didn't have a vehicle on the Navy Yard, I was riding in one that was now stuck there.

As it turned out, the fifth floor of this sanctuary was pretty cold. It was intended to be that way because when you put a lot of bodies into a large room, the room gets pretty warm real fast. However, the side-rooms didn't have that many bodies in it so it was chilly; that included the ante-room where I was. I went downstairs to warm my hands on the glass of the front door. The sun had been warming it for most of the day and the glass felt great. It took a long time for feeling to return to my fingers so I was there for a while. There were contractors there also. They weren't sitting around, but rather standing impatiently waiting to be released so they could get their delivery trucks. They all had their bills of lading with them for the loads they carried, but hadn't been able to deliver, to Building 197, and to their other customers awaiting delivery that day that weren't on the Navy Yard. These contractors' days weren't ending until their loads were all delivered so their day today was going to be a long one because they wouldn't be allowed to pick up their trucks until the next day. Therefore they wouldn't be able to finish their deliveries for today until tomorrow.

One contractor said he had just pulled up to the loading dock with his back gate open when the alarm in the building went off. He was told to leave the area immediately. He left with his gate open and was worried about his cargo. As he discussed his plight with the other contractors, he figured out the authorities would have had to close his gate and pulled his truck out to close the loading dock doors, as was the procedure. All of the contractors had to leave their keys with their vehicles as was also the procedure. Now the announcement that no vehicles would be leaving the Navy Yard tonight didn't settle well with these contractors. After all, their livelihood is based on their delivery schedule, and that was all shot to hell today (no pun intended).

I was at that door long enough to see another building's occupants walk down the middle of the street, past our building to the Conference Center to be interviewed by the FBI. I also overheard that they were looking for another shooter. The FBI pulled up and talked to Captain Theodore to let him know that in time we would be allowed to walk down the street to the conference center like the group we just saw pass by us. There were Marine recruits in the building too. They were attending classes and needed to return to their barracks. They were to be given priority in exiting the building to get to the buses.

To give the Marines priority, the Captain quietly gathered them at the front of the line. He did this quietly so as not to get a riot started with the civilians who were in a rush get out of there. Then he made an announcement for us to prepare to walk to the Conference Center. We were to line up at the front door. The process was to be done in a rather orderly manner. We were told we would each have to wait at the Conference Center to interview with an FBI agent. The line quickly became a mass of people bunched together on the first floor with lines leading up stairwells to each of the floors. The Captain's moving the Marines quietly to the door and then calling the civilians to move to the line at the front door placed the Marines in front and the civilians behind them without causing a disturbance with the civilians. However, the front doors were still not open, and no one was going anywhere.

As the Captain's announcement was being made, people began going down stairs and elevators to get in line to go outside and head to the Conference Center. I got in the mass line on the first floor, but then remembered I needed to call my husband to let him know we were headed to the Conference Center and then by bus to the stadium. After that we were supposed to have rides arranged for us, but there were no guarantees. I returned to the elevator as it was getting ready to head back up to the fifth floor for another load of passengers. As the elevator stopped on the fifth floor and the doors opened, a mass of people started to enter the elevator not expecting anyone to be coming up. When I showed up coming out, it surprised the whole lot of them. They made a hole for me, but not for long. It felt like I was walking through Jell-O and it was filling in around me as I moved forward. As the doors closed there were still people waiting to get in. I knew I'd be in the next group and wouldn't have trouble getting the elevator to stop on the fifth floor again. As I entered the conference ante-room, I noticed the original occupants of the building dragging couches back into offices. Chairs too, were magically disappearing into various offices. By the time I finished my phone call, the hallways were empty of furniture. This was what I expected the building must have looked like before the shooting. I was amazed at the little bit of time it took to get the hallways back in order after we'd started emptying out of the floors.

During my phone call I informed my husband of what I knew, and that I may be late. I enlisted him as a backup just in case I couldn't find a ride home. I knew I could count on him to come and get me. Even if

I didn't feel like picking up my car until the next day, I would at least get home. With that little piece of security tucked in the back of my mind, I didn't mind heading to somewhere I knew nothing about - So now, I was off to the elevator and a line that I knew would eventually walk down the middle of the street to the Conference Center. I walked toward the elevator down what was now a chairless and couchless hallway. It didn't take long to clean up those chairs and move that furniture back to where it belonged.

I entered the elevator for the short ride to the first floor. It stopped on every floor on the way down. There were people waiting for the elevator at every floor and I also observed a line of people waiting to go down the stairs. Of course the line wasn't moving. As the elevator stopped on the first floor and the doors opened I couldn't believe that the line was in the same place it was when I left to go back upstairs to make my telephone call. A man turned to me and told me nothing had moved since I'd left. Then inexplicably, we started moving. It was like the line was waiting for me to return before it would move. I couldn't believe my good fortune.

After leaving a freezing fifth floor, the walk felt good. That was a very short-lived feeling, as I would soon come to find. Though the walk was short enough and felt good, the heat was oppressive. You wouldn't think of a day in the middle of September as being hot and sticky, but this day was. A walk alone would have been OK, but then we had a little bit of a wait on the other end of that walk. Little did I know I'd be standing in a line for a half hour just to get into the Conference Center to wait again, this time, to talk to an FBI agent. Guess that's the government way—hurry up and wait. There were Marines handing out emergency water and I was glad to get some. I didn't realize how thirsty I was until I had a chance to take a sip of that water. Before I knew it, I drank half the bottle. Not knowing where or when I would get water next, I saved the rest.

As the line moved forward, and we got closer to the inside of the conference center, the door was opened and the air conditioning coming out to meet us felt great. I didn't think I'd miss the air conditioning after having been in an icebox all day, but the heat from outside was stifling and I welcomed the inside air. It seemed to me that I flip-flopped from one to the other; almost like the 'grass is greener on the other side' kind of attitude.

Once inside the Conference Center, we lined up along the wall and waited for the next available agent to wave his or her hand to let us know he or she was free. The line went quickly enough. Soon, I was talking to an agent. I told him everything I heard and reminded him that it was all recorded on the 911 tape. It's hard to remember many details when you're diving under a desk, so there wasn't much I could say. Listening to the tapes would provide greater detail. Then he asked me if I saw anything as I was leaving the building. I told him I saw the shattered glass in the front cubicle and the shotgun shell in the last set of cubicles. He asked if I remembered anything else and I told him I'd never forget the smell of gunpowder and the din it cast on the lighting. That was all and I was finished.

I left the Conference Center and boarded a bus that waited until it was filled before it left it's spot. It had to pull up to the front of the line of buses when the first set of buses left. When the driver stepped off the bus for a little bit, more passengers boarded. When someone from the back said that's all, there's no more room, people stopped getting on. Those who got on and were still standing didn't get off though. I can't say that I blamed them either. We were all anxious to get out of there.

I could see a traffic officer motioning the bus to move out and since the bus wasn't moving, he came over to find out why. When he looked in and saw no driver he explained to those of us sitting in front that he was motioning the bus to move, but now he knew why it wasn't moving. He asked us where the driver went. Since the driver didn't tell us where he was going when he left, we told him we didn't' know. We told him that since he was a Marine, he took his hat with him. So, off he went in search of a Marine. Soon the driver and the traffic officer came back. The officer directed our bus down the exit road and then motioned to incoming busses to circle around him to approach the front of the Conference Center. We drove out the gate onto an empty street along with a police escort.

Through the front windshield of the bus, as we drove out the front gate and on to M Street with a police escort. I saw that the only cars around were marked and unmarked police cars, and they were parked in the street with lights flashing. At one point there was a one block section of the right side of the road cordoned off for cameras. Our police escort moved to the left side of the road for that block to avoid the cameras and camera crews, and then moved back to the right side. Our bus followed suit. Eventually, our bus turned toward the National's stadium, passing around the East and South side to swing around the West side and turn into the North side road, where only buses were permitted entrance. The roads we traveled, the entire route, was occupied with only marked and unmarked police cars, lights flashing, parked in the street. There were no civilian cars along the route at all.

We off-loaded and immediately were handed bottled water again. Even though I still had a half finished bottle, I opened this one. It was cooler water and I drank half of it before taking another step.

From the bus, we were sent into a line where the Red Cross had food waiting for us. Even though Captain Theodore's group fed us what they had on hand in the morning, a meal was very welcome right now. It was about 1900 now and we'd gone a long time without a regular full meal, most of us since our 0630 start time. Just as I was getting situated, one of the Navy officers yelled out that a bus was loading up and heading to Stafford, Virginia. When I heard that, I butted the food line and grabbed a couple of sandwiches. Then I rushed over to the officer to make sure I'd find out which was the right bus heading to Stafford. I didn't want to catch the wrong one. The officer pointed to the intended bus, but the bus driver said he hadn't been tasked with a run to Stafford. This puzzled me and made me just a little irritated because I'd just butted a line to grab something to eat while traveling to Stafford. I went back inside the gate and started to sit down, but then saw someone with Red Cross blankets. It was getting cooler and as this was turning into a long night, I thought it might be a good idea to get one. I asked the lady with the blanket where she had gotten it from and she pointed me to the volunteer with boxes of blankets. I promptly went over to ask for one and she handed it to me with a comforting smile. I needed that after what I'd just been through, cutting a line, running to catch a non-existent bus, and finding myself back at the beginning with my bottle of water and at least some food to eat. After thinking I'd get a ride to Stafford and finding out that wasn't the case, I figured that blanket would keep me warm during what was turning out to be a very long night. I then settled in to eat my two little sandwiches; and I have to tell you, they tasted delicious. Thank you Red Cross!

The officer who told me the bus would be leaving to Stafford tracked me down to apologize for giving me incorrect information. He was told a bus would be leaving for Stafford and made the assumption it was the bus that just came in. He told me he was working on getting a task order for a bus to head to Stafford and he'd let me know when that was complete. I told him I understood. This was a new experience for all of us and there were a few systemic bugs to work out. In my mind, one of the bugs to work out would be to better optimize the use of buses. It doesn't make much sense to task a bus to travel all the way to Stafford until everyone who is headed to Stafford is present and ready to go. To me it would be wasteful to send a bus out with only some of the people on board who needed to go where it was headed. Stafford is such a long way and one bus load would probably handle the trip. Two runs would just be a waste of valuable and costly resources. On any account, I thanked him for looking me up and explaining what happened. By now, I was finishing up my sandwiches and since I now had time, I thought it prudent to go back and dig into some salad and ziti since it would likely be several more hours until transportation could be arranged for people heading to Stafford. I did this and it felt good to eat a balanced meal that included something hot, even if it was this late at night.

Having satisfied my nagging hunger, I went outside the gate on the sidewalk to find the Stafford sign and wait for a ride. Any kind of a ride would sure be good right about now. As I walked by a table, someone said something about, "…if you need to talk about your experience we're here for you or we can get you in touch with someone." I couldn't help myself when I said, "I just may need to talk to someone," but moved on down the sidewalk to find the Stafford sign. I sat down to wait and got out some paperwork to read over. Just as soon as I settled down, a fellow came to stand next to me and bent over to speak quietly to me. He said that he's a certified counselor and he really meant it when he said his group was here to talk to victims.

This set me back a little. I thought he was either a walking advertisement for a counseling center, or was there to let us know there were counseling services available. I certainly never expected him to follow up. I thought he was just being nice when he was standing at the table collecting names of those who wanted to talk. Since he wasn't pushy at the table I gave it little thought until he showed up where I was sitting.

He asked if I minded talking to him. I told him I didn't care who I talked to. He asked if I would follow him so we could find somewhere where we could talk that was a little less public; so I did. We stood there around the corner from the mass of people offloading from the buses and walking around waiting, and talking, and waiting. He asked me what was wrong, and that is when I lost it. I managed to keep myself together the entire day until now. Now that we were safe and out of the Yard, I could express the bottled up fear I had kept inside me the entire day from the first gunshot to the last step off the bus here.

It started with the frustration of not being able to pinpoint the shooter sufficiently enough for the police so they could find him right away. The frustration at the police actually trying to take him alive instead of taking him down. I still don't understand the mentality of police identification and the "put your hands up!" phrasing when pursuing a killer. What were they thinking? Did they think a shooter was actually going to put his hands up? Well, he didn't give up. He just kept killing people. The frustration at the police for not realizing that he'd already killed, so another one or two kills was just icing on the cake for him. Why the heck didn't they take the situation more seriously before those kills occurred and just end it?

After all, I sat under my desk giving locations to the 911 operator based on where the shots I heard came from and the police found and lost him so many times. I just couldn't believe it! What was up with that? Didn't we have our own guards in on that operation? Our guards would know their way around the building because they walk it daily. Why didn't the police use guards who knew the building layout? It's as if each police agency wanted to take credit for subduing the shooter and hauling him in front of the cameras for the public to see.

Then there was the frustration of not being able to find my employees, my co-workers, and my supervisor. The things I heard during the shooting spree, giving the 911 operator directions to the gunshots, and then finding out how he cruelly blew away his victims—just snuffing their lives out without giving it a second thought—frustrates me to tears. Then I started blurting out things I could have, should have done. Why couldn't I have just grabbed a chair right after one of his shots and pushed it into him from behind to take him off guard? At the very beginning, it would have been a shock to him because he wouldn't have expected it, not until the police came would he have expected something like that. I explained that pushing him like that probably would have enabled someone else to grab his weapon. It would have been over so much faster—with so many more lives saved. Why?

The counselor tried to say the right things to make me feel better. At the time it helped for a few minutes. Then someone said there was a car leaving for Stafford. I thanked him and ran to catch the ride. These thoughts are still on my mind today even though I know hind sight is 20-20, and if I did shove a chair at the shooter I would most likely be dead, but would the rest of those who were killed that day also be dead?

CHAPTER 8

Getting Home

Let me go back to "There isn't even a task order for transportation to Stafford, Virginia yet." It was working up to being a very long night. It seems the bus option was always going to be available, but I could see how this was going to play out. Getting a bus was going to take a while. Even though I knew it didn't take much to have a task order drawn up, I was wondering how long it would be before a bus tasking would be changed to ferrying people down south instead of from the Navy Yard to the Stadium. I could see I would be in for a long wait.

Ubercars to the rescue! Ubercars is a unique car company in the DC area. They provide transportation services by matching drivers and cars at an extremely competitive rate. Tonight Ubercars provided free rides to commuter lots for those stranded by the horrific event at the Navy Yard. The Ubercars representatives were at the corner of the stadium and taking signups for rides to the various commuter lot areas. All the company needed was one person's name to put against the car so they could show it was used to transport someone from the Navy Yard event. Once they had someone signed up to go somewhere, they waited until they had enough passengers to fill a car. Then they would dispatch a car to make the drive to the destination. Someone had already signed for a ride to Dale City, which is halfway to Stafford. There were three of us who needed to go further down. One rider needed to go to the Minnieville Road commuter lot. I and another rider needed to go to the Stafford commuter lot.

The assigned car had already arrived, but it was across the street on the west side of the National's Stadium. It looked like the driver was ready to leave so we ran for the car. Wouldn't you know it? When we tried to cross the street, the light turned, but there was no walk light for us. The driver got in the car and we all yelled at him to wait and don't go. Then we didn't even wait for the light. We just waited for the traffic to clear and we ran half way across to the median strip against the light. Then when the other side was clear, we ran the rest of the way across, against the light. We weren't about to lose our ride!

We all hopped in, but the driver opened the trunk for my bag and laptop. That dreaded laptop. I'll get to that later. The driver got onto I-95 and headed south. Giving the driver directions to the first stop was pretty straight-forward. This commuter lot was located right off the highway. After dropping off the person in the front seat to that lot, I moved to the front seat to make more room in the back seat for the other two passengers.

The next drop off was Minneville road. It was the destination for the lady in the back and it was up to her to provide the driver with directions. At night it's a different trip than during the day, especially when you aren't the one driving from the Navy Yard during the trip home. It was difficult for her to give directions, and even more difficult for her to give directions to the driver to send him back to the highway again after being dropped off. As it turns out, her directions got us lost. Finally, we pulled off the road to let the man in the back seat have his address entered into the driver's GPS. He was headed south to Stafford and his address provided the driver with GPS directions back to the highway. Sure enough, the driver had to make a U turn and head back toward the lighted businesses and eateries that we'd come through. That made sense because they would be located closer to the highway rather than farther from it.

The next stop was the Mine Road commuter lot in Stafford. It was becoming obvious that the driver was getting frustrated with having to make so many stops just to drop off a single person even though this was only the second person he was taking to a commuter lot. When I said I needed to go to the 630 commuter lot, the man in the back seat offered to take me to my lot. I gratefully accepted knowing the driver would take me to my lot but would really rather not. After all, Ubercars was doing this for us as a courtesy and I felt it wasn't fair to make him have to drive me even farther down the highway. The man in the back seat warned me that he drove an old work truck, but I told him I didn't care as long as we didn't have to push it. He chuckled and said he kept it in good mechanical shape. That was all I cared about. When the driver got to Mine Road, we just had him stop at the truck in one of the first rows so he could easily turn around and head back out of the lot. The work truck was one of the last vehicles still left on the lot. It looked to me like there were probably a few more people who needed to come down here from the Navy Yard because there were a few more cars left in the lot. We thanked the driver, and I asked for a card, but he didn't have one. I intended to write a note of thanks to Ubercars for their generosity in our time of need.

When we got to the truck, the man, I still don't know his name, started clearing out the passenger seat and put it in the bed of the truck. It looked to me like he was going to clear the whole front seat. I told him he didn't need to be doing that unless there was something fragile on the seat that I might break. He said he was just clearing off enough room so I could sit down. He'd already put his briefcase in on the other side of the cloth "stuff" and moved some of the stuff from the front seat, but I slipped in and grabbed the "stuff," briefcase and all so he could get in on his side. I again told him I sat in much worse and he didn't need to clear it for me. He said no one ever sits on that side so he never cleans it off. He took me down the back road from the Mine Road lot to the 630 lot and right up to my car. When I got out he took the stuff out of the bed of his truck where he put it when he started to clear the front seat and put it back in the front seat. Then he waited for me to start my car and put it in gear before he pulled away. He was a gentleman to the fullest by making sure I got off all right.

    I got out of the lot and onto the road and drove. For the first time I drove slowly, which is a big change for me. On the way home I was thinking that this day would take some time to get over. I had a hunch I would be in for a difficult time over the next few weeks. I didn't look forward to it either. As it turned out, my prediction would be right on target. When I got home, it was 2200 and I talked to my sweetie about the day's events. I told him everything that went on, the gunshots, the shattered glass, the pall of gunpowder dimming the lighting to a gray-blue hue, not finding anyone from my department, or my floor for hours and then having to call 911 back to get someone to go into Building 197 to pull out my supervisor and co-workers. Then the long time it took to track down my employee. Oh, God, I thought she was dead when I couldn't find her. I still remember that aching feeling and it still sends shivers down my spine like it just happened yesterday; seeing her head back to where she encountered that shooter; hearing the shot. Then thinking she is lying dead; not seeing blood or her as I was being guided out by the policeman; not knowing, just simply not knowing. It comes back to me that I didn't act fast enough to drag her back with me and save her. Those few minutes, hours, come back. The interminable time I sat there not moving while the shooter stood right behind me. All of it; he heard it all. Now that it was about 0100 in the morning, I was famished again. I realized it had been six hours since I'd last eaten. My hubby cooked up a hamburger for me; a big one;

and I ate the whole thing. At this hour of the evening, or should I say morning, I was surprised that I ate the whole thing!

I had a glass of wine with the hamburger, and then another glass just for the hell of it. I thought I'd need that wine to help me sleep after what I went through today. I had a third glass, but this time, just for good measure, I added a shot, or was it two, of American Honey whiskey. I was determined to get some sleep. I didn't. I woke up almost every hour on the hour. It was the same nightmare, varying slightly but similar enough to call it the same. In each one I woke up just before I die so I never see exactly how I die, I just know the end result is; I die.

CHAPTER 9

I Need Help!

"Thank God I located Nina! She's safe." Having found Nina after so many hours of searching was a relief. I gave her a couple of days to spend with her child, and then called her to find out how she was. I got her voicemail and left a message that we had to talk. I'm not sure how she would take that, but I really did have to talk to her. I was so elated that she was physically alright. However, if I was feeling the way I was and I wasn't even shot at, I had to ask her how she felt, really felt. After all, she faced the shooter, had a gun aimed at her, and was shot at. She looked into that killer's eyes and knew he was intending to kill her. If she wasn't a track star and in physically great shape, she would be dead now, and she knows it. I had to see if she was going to get help. She'd been through a terrible ordeal.

Nina called the following morning to let me know she got out of the building with Russ after she left my cubicle. I told her I tried to grab her but she left before I could even lunge forward. I also told her I thought she was heading right back into danger when she headed toward the shooter's last known location. So, when I couldn't find her during all those hours of searching, I was becoming acutely aware that she may have been shot trying to escape because she just happened to turn the wrong way in her haste to get out of the building. She explained to me about running into Russ and his grabbing her hand and running down the middle set of stairs and to the atrium. She also explained that at that point, she and Russ split up. She said that she headed for the front door while providing a description and location of the shooter to the guards; and all of that without breaking her stride. She said she found herself zigzagging through the atrium and in such a rush to get out the front door she didn't notice it was locked. Even as the police and guards were telling her she couldn't go out the front, she continued yelling the description and location as she ran past the guards and out the front door. Hearing she was safe and how she got out made my heart leap, and I never tire of hearing her description of that part of her escapade. We contacted each other over the next couple of days to make sure we were each okay. Of course, we weren't, but it helped to talk to each other.

During one of our calls, I told Nina about my dreams and she gave me the number for the crisis center. After her experience, the FBI put her in touch with a counselor almost immediately. So now she was sharing this information with me because I knew I needed help and had no idea where to turn. I'm so glad she had those phone numbers. Until I could get in touch with them, she also gave me the Civilian Employee Assistance Program (CEAP) counselor main number.

I called the CEAP number and they got me in touch with a counselor in my area. I went to see the counselor and it felt good to talk to someone, but it didn't stop my nightmares. There were some moments when I didn't feel like this counselor was used to talking to people who'd been through a traumatic situation. But it did feel good to talk. I knew I still needed to talk to someone who could help me get over my nightmares and to help me get some sleep. Waking every hour during the first few nights after the shooting was leaving me totally exhausted. I needed some help to get some sleep so I could start the healing process. Until now, everything I was trying and all the counselors I was seeing, I was doing on my own.

I looked on my insurer's webpage (Tricare) for psychiatrists and found two in my local area. I called the first one and was told that the web page is outdated because that person left over a year ago. Wow! What a way to talk to someone seeking psychological help. I called the second number and gave the receptionist my information, which she said she would give to the psychiatrist and then get back to me. I called again later that afternoon and the secretary said the doctor still has the information.

The first day went by and no return call. About mid-morning on the second day I called and talked to the secretary again. She told me the doctor still hadn't gotten back to her. Questions are going off in my head now. I waited. Later in the afternoon, I called the secretary again and she told me the doctor still hasn't decided yet. This set me back. I didn't say anything about that, but thanked the secretary and hung up. I haven't called back since that day. A psychiatrist who is on our insurance provider list and is listed as taking new female patients needs to decide about taking me? There is something wrong with this picture. I'm already experiencing a myriad of feelings and can't distinguish where one is separated from the other; they seem to mix together in layers rather than cued end to end in linear fashion. Among those feelings is frustration and the very person who should be helping me is causing even more frustration. Now, I'm in a downward spiral.

During a previous call with Nina, she told me the crisis center mentioned forms to fill out to continue getting paid until she could get herself together enough to get back to work. She talked to our Human Relations (HR) department and was sent the forms. We spoke on the phone just a few times in between the counseling, physical therapy for my shoulder, and psychiatrist sessions, but it felt so good to hear her voice. She sent me an email telling me she didn't want to push anything on me. She asked if I wanted her to forward those forms to me. She said at least then I'd have them in my inbox and could take my time making the decision about whether I wanted to fill them out or not. She also said our HR point of contact, would be able to take them and file them for us. I said yes to those forms.

Nina gave me the phone numbers to HR so I could get assistance with the forms if I needed it. Our HR contact then called to let me know the forms would be coming to me that day; and only one form had to be filed right away, but the other would eventually also have to be filed, just not immediately. I thanked her, and within the hour, an email arrived with the forms. I looked back at the numbers Nina gave me and saw a Department of Labor number and reference to claim forms so this must be what Nina was referring to. In the email our HR representative explained to me what needed to be filled in and what needed to be left blank. I followed her directions. The explanation about which numbers not to fill in was critical because they had to have specific wording in them. I found there is a claims examiner who looks over the Workman's Compensation claims and could deny a claim because the explanation was incorrectly written. I began filling out one form that had to be sent in right away. The other form was for the doctor and I would have to remember to get that to him at my next visit.

Nina had faced a real crisis and lived to tell about it so the FBI made sure she had all the numbers to access any help she needed. When she passed some of those numbers on to me, I knew it was for a service that could help me in one way or another. I looked up some of those numbers and found the crisis center number. They talked to me for about an hour and said they would work on getting me in to see a psychiatrist. This was encouraging. After all, I still hadn't called back the psychiatrists office that hadn't "made a decision yet" on whether to take me or not even though the web page said she was taking new female patients.

My supervisor called early in the morning of 19 September to make sure I was okay. We talked a little and she told me she was coming to my house. Apparently I still didn't sound okay to her. I gave her my address so she could put it into her GPS. Then I started straightening out the house. I didn't feel like cleaning up in my present state; it was all I could do to get up and eat. I was so exhausted all I wanted to do was just to go back to bed. One thing I did do well however, was eat. It was so easy to do. I only wish I could be served my food in my chair instead of having to get up and walk to the table. I'm guessing my body wanted to eat to relieve some of the tension. Then my boss called to let me know she was on her way, but there was a closed road blocking her from getting through. This confused me because there were no closed roads anywhere. When she read off the names of the roads nearby, none of them sounded familiar.

I knew she must have keyed the name of one of the roads wrong but I had no clue. The easiest way out of the mess she was in was to get her back out to the main highway and start her over from there. Once we got her back out to the main road, she made her way to the "end state maintenance" line that begins the gravel roadway to my house. She continued toward the big pond I told her about until she saw the roadsign to my cul de sac and my driveway leading to my residence. At the cul de sac at the end of the gravel roadway she spotted my address on the fence post. This was the entrance to my yard.

When I heard knocking on the garage door, I assumed my hubby had his hands full and couldn't open the garage door. By that time I was already on the front porch looking for Jill's car. When I opened the front door and didn't see Jill but saw her car sitting in the drive, I thought maybe hubby grabbed her to show off some of the things he was working on. So, I started around toward the garage to find them. However, the knocking sound was Jill who'd come to the garage door instead of the front door. When I saw her, and she saw me, we met in the middle of the garage and hugged. This is about the time my husband walked out of his workshop, which is next to the garage. I introduced Jill to him and he left us alone so we could talk. Then Jill turned around to look at the pond, canoe, grape vines growing on the fence, heron flying away from the pond, and forest surrounding us and told me that I live in heaven. I agreed and said the commute is tough, but this is what I come home to each day. Then I told her she needed to see the back yard.

We walked inside and Jill commented on the Christmas gifts that were wrapped and sitting on the floor. I spent the previous Sunday wrapping Christmas gifts in preparation for mailing them off to family members. I told her they were waiting for bows and my next weekend's job was supposed to be making and placing the bows on the packages, but that my planning may have some hiccups in it now. We sat down next to each other on the couch in the living room to talk.

Jill wanted to know how I was doing. I know she was suffering as much if not more, than me, but her interest was in finding out how I was doing. She said Shellie, her new boss, was worried about me too. I told Jill about my nightmares and how they always seemed to end the same way. I end up dying, but I wake up before I die so I never actually see myself die. I start myself awake with a jerk and don't understand how my husband isn't awakened by this because, to me anyway, it seems like I jump in the air with that start.

I told Jill that I cry even talking about the nightmares. I cry talking about thinking of Nina having been shot during the hours right after the shooting when I couldn't find her. Jill said she couldn't believe I tried to muster everyone. I felt I just had to get a grip on something, even if it was just accounting for everyone. Jill asked if I had the crisis center's number. I got up and brought the phone book back to look and make sure one of the numbers I wrote on the back when talking to Nina was the crises center number. Jill asked if I had any paper and

I sent her into my husband's den to get paper from his printer. She said, "You each have your own den?" My response was, "Yes, there isn't enough room in one den for the two of us." She had me copy her phone number so I could call her anytime from the house phone and not have to look up her number in my cell phone (we don't get cell service inside the house). She had me transfer the phone numbers from the phone book's front cover to the little booklet she made for me from the paper she grabbed off of the printer. She said it was simple, but effective and all the numbers I needed would be in one place. She said I also needed to put my appointment schedules with each counselor in the booklet. That way I wouldn't have to keep track of a little appointment card and then fly into a hissy fit when I misplaced it. I said something to the effect of, "Sounds like you've been in this kind of situation before." Jill said I needed to get some valium prescribed so I could get some sleep. You'd have to know Jill to understand why she would need a valium to calm her down and why nothing else would work.

It seems like we just sat down to talk and Jill was just getting me organized when the phone rang. It was the crisis center. They'd found a psychiatrist who could see me at 1:30 that day at Walter Reed in Bethesda, Maryland. It was a little after noon now. This meant I'd have to hurry to make it there by 1:30. It was normally a two hour drive. Since I'd just taken some medication that helped to make me sleepy, Jill wanted to make sure I didn't fall asleep while traveling to Walter Reed. So, she wanted to make me a cup of coffee to drink during the drive. She walked into the kitchen and saw 3 coffee makers. I showed her the coffee maker that works fastest because it makes hot water and you can use instant coffee. She poured water in the top of the coffee maker while I handed her a travel mug. She put the coffee and Splenda in the mug while the hot water was heating. I gathered my phone, purse and wallet to make sure I had my ID and came back for the coffee.

I thanked Jill for coming and she shooed me out of the house. She said she'd follow me to the highway. I don't think she took into account my driving habits because I left her in my dust. I was in a hurry; I really didn't want to miss this appointment. Even though I was late, the psychiatrist seemed to know I would be, and he held a slot open for me. It helped to talk to a psychiatrist not only because he seemed to know what I was talking about, but he also seemed to know what I was feeling. He appeared to "get it." He also prescribed a short term sleep aid.

The short term sleep aid helped me get through the night without waking up every hour on my way to my death. I was greatly encouraged the first night. I actually slept most of the night and only got up once. Even then, I went back to sleep and slept the rest of the night. That was a wonderful feeling, to sleep. I was looking forward to getting caught up on sleep. The second night wasn't very successful. I don't know what happened. I couldn't get to sleep. I was shivering, not continuously, but sporadically. Nonetheless, I was shivering and couldn't stop long enough to get to sleep. I pulled the coverlet over me, so now I had the blanket and quilted coverlet on top of me and I was still shivering. It wasn't cold in the house, but I couldn't stop shivering. I drank some hot cocoa and tried to go to sleep again. When again I couldn't get to sleep, I drank some wine and tried it again, and again. Then I added some wiskey to my wine and tried to sleep again. This time, instead of lying in bed shivering and taking the chance that I would wake my husband, I grabbed my pillow and went to the living room to sit in my recliner. I covered up with my fuzzy blanket and sat there with my feet up and pillow behind me. This always seemed to work in the past, so I was hoping to get some sleep before morning. At some time between 0400 and 0500, I must have dozed off because the next thing I knew, I opened my eyes and looked at the clock. It was 0700. Not a full night's rest, but a few hours were better than none.

CHAPTER 10

What were They Thinking?

"On September 16, 2013, Aaron Alexis, a lone gunman armed initially with a shotgun, fatally shot twelve people and injured three others in a mass shooting at the headquarters of the Naval Sea Systems Command (NAVSEA) inside the Washington Navy Yard in Southeast Washington, D.C. The attack began around 8:20 a.m. EDT in Building 197. Alexis was killed by police around 9:20 a.m. EDT."[5]

Official reports state Alexis came to Washington, DC on August 25, 2013 and had been staying in hotels in the days leading up to the shooting. His job required him to move about the country as part of his contract work. This included work from New England to North Carolina. He switched hotels several times until September 7, when he finally settled into the Residence Inn, which was within a mile of the Navy Yard.

Over the past few days we were finding out more about the shooter through the news. People in the city of Fort Worth, who knew him and frequented the same places he did, were interviewed. In fact, his landlord told newspaper reporters that Aaron Alexis was a "sweet and

---

[5] Washington Post headlines, October 16, 2013.

intelligent guy." He referred to him as a kind man who was always ready to help someone out any time he was asked. Others said he could never harm anyone. They described him as always looking for the good in people even those who were gruff and short with other people. Alexis was described as someone who occasionally joined Thai immigrants in meditation at a local Buddhist temple. This person they were describing didn't even sound like the same man who terrorized the people in Building 197 that Monday morning. How could a man buy a shotgun, take it with him to work, look people straight in the eye, and shoot them? How could the man they were describing shoot at anyone, period?[6]

When I started setting pen to paper in an effort to tell my story, several other stories came through, and not all are complete yet, including mine. One of the purposes of my story was to identify flaws between what media was telling and what I led myself to believe based on what I observed during an incident that happened going through our "scanners." When I escorted an instructor through the "scanners" and the alarm went off, I assumed it was because he was wheeling his metal framed case through the turnstyle. I made the connection between the turnstyles we went through and the alarm going off when the instructor's case went through as metal detectors in the turnstyles. For this reason, I had to ask when setting up the security system, what was the thinking in setting up waist-high metal detector scanners when other government buildings have whole body metal detectors? What was the thinking behind this decision? Yes, many government buildings allow employees free access to bring in whatever they want and visitors

---

[6] It was reported Aaron Alexis purchased a Remington 870 Express Tactical 12-gauge shotgun two days before the shooting from a gun shop in Virginia. It was etched with messages including "My ELF Weapon!" which police believe was an apparent reference to extremely low-frequency waves. Also etched on the weapon were the words, "End to The Torment!"

are scanned. This would not have helped find the gun in the shooter's bag, or under his arm and down his side, behind his bag, whichever the case. The problem doesn't lie in the scanner. But having the scanner be a real scanner would have been the final step in a series of systems that could have stopped him when all the other systems in place failed.

All employees and visitors have to pass through a waist-high "sensor" instead of a metal detector, as we swipe our CACs to enter the building. Apparently the sensor is set to only pick up electronic equipment in wheeled carts that people drag along behind them as they walk through the gate that opens with the "key" on the CAC. The video released by the FBI shows the shooter walking into the front doors where he obviously passed through one of those waist-high "sensors." He must have figured that he could sneak a weapon either in his back pack casually slung over his shoulder—just like dozens of other people entering the building do with their bags on a daily basis, or held under his arm and down his side since the "sensor" wouldn't pick up the metal. There his demeanor in the videos didn't hint of a crazed man who would, within the hour, kill 12 people before his rampage was finally ended by the police.

One clue to Alexis' potential for violence was a statement made by a lay worker at the Buddhist temple who said, "He could be very aggressive." This behavior could escalate his mannerism into someone who had the potential to one day kill himself. Newspaper stories about him reported that he had two previous incidents with police over firearms violations. Yet this man was able to get a secret clearance and was issued a CAC. This allowed him free access to the building. How he got the gun into the building is also hard to believe.

There were a number of other incidents that indicated critical system failures. For instance, Alexis had a number of run-ins with the law resulting from civil disturbances. Background checks on Aaron Alexis showed that he was arrested in 2004 in Seattle, Washington, for malicious mischief after shooting out the tires of a vehicle during a bout of road rage. In 2008 he was arrested by DeKalb County, Georgia officials for disorderly conduct. It should be noted that none of his arrests led to prosecution.

According to Navy officials, Alexis was also cited on at least eight occasions for misconduct while serving on active duty. In 2010 he was arrested for discharging a weapon within Fort Worth city limits, a fact Alexis did not report on his security clearance application forms at the Navy Yard. It was also apparently overlooked by federal government background investigations. Newspaper editorials report that The Experts, the company he worked for at the Navy Yard, ran two background checks on Alexis and identified only a traffic violation. The same reports indicate that the Pentagon confirmed twice that Alexis had a valid security clearance. Finally, it was reported that his federal personnel report failed to mention his arrest in 2004.

Then there were the numerous warnings that Alexis suffered from mental health issues. Again, newspaper reports indicate Alexis was suffering from some sort of mental illness. One example was the police report he filed in Rhode Island on August 2, 2013 in which he claimed to be the victim of harassment. He also reported hearing voices in his head. According to FBI files released to the public, Alexis had delusional beliefs that he was being controlled or influenced by extremely low frequency electromagnetic waves. In fact, federal authorities discovered statements on Alexis' thumb drives, phones, and computers where he proclaimed, "Ultra low frequency attack is what I've been subject to for the last 3 months. And to be perfectly honest, that is what has driven me to this."[7]

---

[7] The FBI reported in an AP press release that a note left behind and found by investigators after the shooting, that he was driven to the shooting rampage because he was being bombarded by extremely low-frequency radio waves. The FBI said that the note, along with peculiar carved notations on his shotgun, suggested he was in an agonizing struggle with profound paranoia and delusions.

It was reported that after the Rhode Island incident, Alexis was prescribed Trazodone for his insomnia. Then, about two weeks later he showed up at the emergency rooms of two Veterans Affairs hospitals where he was again prescribed Trazadone, and subsequently had refilled on a second visit.

More recently, police were called to answer a complaint at the Virginia hotel where Alexis was staying. Alexis apparently told police that he, "believed people were following him and using a microwave machine to send vibrations into his body so he could not fall asleep. Police then report that they alerted the Navy Yard that day that Alexis was hearing voices. It appears that the information was not acted upon by the Navy base.

Shortly after the Navy Yard shooting incident, the Washington (AP) reported that according to officials following the Navy investigation, The Experts, the company that employed Alexis, pulled his access to classified material for two days, from August 7 to August 9, when mental health problems became evident. The company also restored his access rights soon thereafter, did not record nor explain their decision, and never informed the Navy about the withdrawal as required by law. This all occurred during the time Alexis called Newport, Rhode Island police complaining about voices that were harassing him through the wall of his hotel room where he was staying.

How did all these apparent breaches in security just "slip" through the crack? Since the shooting spree, the Navy and Defense Department initiated several "reviews" into base security and contractor requirements focusing closely on background security checks. Why does all this happen after the fact? Where is the IG or GAO during all these lapses? Why do people always have to die before the government takes action? I guess my main question though would be if the security officers at the front door can make you hand over and secure personal cell phones, why can't they do the same for weapons? How do weapons get through security in the first place?

This man had problems with the law and was allowed to get, and keep his security clearance. There is something wrong with this picture alone; but there's more. Problems with the law and involving a gun are a red flag. This man didn't have one problem with the law, he had two and both were involving a gun. That alone should have been enough to never have gotten his security clearance to even have had it revoked. Oddly enough, nothing was done to track those two problems he had with a gun. Perhaps his employer at the time wasn't notified. Perhaps Alexis put on a great act of regret, telling the police his gun went off accidentally. We may never know. When he managed to get this position with the contractor and was placed at the Navy Yard, what did his employer do to ensure his security clearance was not compromised? Is Alexis' continuing to hold a security clearance a result of that systemic problem, or is it a result of an interim clearance pending a full security clearance review that wasn't complete enough? Either way, what is wrong with that picture? The problem here is systemic.

Having only been on the job a month and having his manager talk to him about his conduct or performance, whichever, should have also been a red flag. One who was brought from the outside to perform specific tasks should not only perform the tasks, but also be able to get along with others well enough that he doesn't have complaints lodged against him within a month of his arrival on the job. Even though that was just the week prior, the incident had to be coming to a head, long before then.

The events of this day can't be blamed on a sudden change of demeanor on the part of the shooter. In spite of the fact that he bought the weapon just two days before his shooting spree, he had to have been planning this for longer than that; he needed to know where to put his weapon together undisturbed, and which direction to head once he left the bathroom. He had planned well, and gone far before finally being taken down by the police. According to a 31-second video released by the FBI, the shooter arrived at work at 7:53 a.m. in his blue Toyota Prius rental car where he parked it in Parking Garage #28. At 8:08 a.m. he then proceeded to Building 197 where he entered the front doors carrying a backpack slung over his left shoulder and proceded through security. Once in the building, he headed directly to the elevators.

At 8:09 a.m. he exited the elevator on the fourth floor where he turned left and entered the men's bathroom in the east area (the newer part of the building) carrying the backpack and a clipboard. The police then report that at 8:15 a.m. the shooter left the bathroom and crossed the hallway to the West area nearest the bathroom with a shotgun but without the other items he had carried into the bathroom. Major news outlets reported on Monday that Alexis used an AR-15, but this was not the case. The sounds of the weapon were more like those of a shotgun, not an AR-15. Also, from my point of view, he had to have left the bathroom and headed into the East area, where he would have found easy targets in a man who was shoving a woman into a cubicle. He would have shot those two people together then turned to leave the edges of the cubicle area and head toward the West area of the fourth floor, shooting the supervisor who entered the bathroom area to investigate the noise; then he continued to the West area, shooting his third person who sat in the corner cubicle at the end of the row as he entered the West side cubicles. According to reports, Aaron Alexis shot his first victim at 8:16 a.m. The 911 tapes indicate the first calls for assistance from the fourth floor began arriving at approximately 8:17 a.m. My call was answered by the 911 operator at about 8:17. He then turned and walked toward our area through the kitchen hallway, saw Jill turn and run and saw my employee attempting to hide. When he closed in on my employee, he raised his shotgun at close range and shot at her. Then he walked toward the back hallway and shot at Joel's employee, Russ. (who jumped over and into the cubicle behind his) as he headed toward the banister overlooking the atrium to shoot down into the atrium, before turning and heading back up the row toward the front hallway and the stairs.

The picture released by the government to the FBI and public, at Figure 2, shows Alexis going down the center east stairwell on the East wing from the fourth to the third floor and slinking through the stairwell doorway into the front hallway holding his shotgun at the ready.

Figure 2. Aaron Alexis heading into the third floor from the building's central stairwell.

Security videos show that at about 8:20 a.m. the shooter left the fourth floor. That means that in a five minute period he killed 4 people, and shot at two more people on just one floor. The third floor wall straight down the stairs from our area has a bulletin board right across from the stairwell with Team Ships notices. It can be seen in Figure 2 with the shooter going through the doorway of the stairwell into the third floor from the fourth floor. He used the stairway to decend to the third floor instead of the elevators so he could see any activity that might be going on while he was descending.

Shortly thereafter the security video shows him next on the first floor at 8:28 a.m. then again on the third floor at 8:57 a.m. This matches up with my reports of his locations to the 911 operator so she could relay that information to the police who were looking for him in the building. In Figure 3, the shooter can be seen on the third floor hiding from the view of the people at the end of the hallway.

Figure 3. Shooter looking down hallway at people at end of hallway.

The shooter entered the third floor and was preparing to find more people to shoot. After the first two "Fourth floor," "[unintelligible mutterings]" and shots, I heard no more utterings associated with his shots. Without access to the entire length of video, it is difficult to say how long he spends looking for those particular people. However, I counted several single shots from the general area where the people are seen in this photo on the third floor. I have no knowledge of any particular individuals on the first floor who were killed; I just know the shooter fired his weapon at individuals while he was down there.

In this case, he hid until he found people to shoot, and then clandestinely slinked down the hallway in the direction of his next targets, the people he saw at the end of the hallway in Figure 4. He was looking for those people he saw from his hiding position.

Figure 4. Shooter then heading to the end of the hallway toward his targets.

To put the shooting and timeline into perspective, between 8:17 a.m. and 9:25 a.m. the shooter shot and killed another 11 people including one police officer, and wounded a number of others; three critically. Finally, at 9:25 a.m. the shooter is killed by police during what can only be described as a wild shootout.

My question is; why didn't someone notice Alexis when he first entered the men's bathroom? Why didn't someone notice a man carrying a shotgun down the hallway toward the first row of cubicles? We aren't crowded, but we have enough people walking around that someone should have noticed a single black man, very unusually and casually dressed, out of place on our floor, wielding a weapon. As a matter of fact, we have cameras all over the place. We have all those cameras, again, providing a feeling of security, yet no one was watching those cameras to notice a man walking around shooting people on three different floors! How many people's lives could have been saved had there been monitored cameras instead of unmonitored cameras?

The shooter stayed close to the central and north parts of Building 197 and remained on the fourth floor, first floor, and a little of the third floor during the majority of his shooting spree. That was obvious even without my guiding the 911 operator by the sounds of the shots. The police could have handed over this information to the FBI. The building's cameras told the story of his travels.

CHAPTER 11

Memorial Services

On Sunday, September 22, 2013, President Barack Obama, Department of Defense Secretary Chuck Hagel, Secretary of the Navy Ray Mabus, Admirals Greenert and Hilarides, Washington DC Mayor Gray, leaders from across the city and our Armed Forces, came to pay tribute to all the outstanding first responders and the families of those who lost loved ones during the September 16, 2013 shooting spree at the Navy Yard. President Obama was addressing the attendees, "We know that no words we offer today are equal to the magnitude, to the depths of that loss. But we come together as a grateful nation to honor your loved ones, to grieve with you, and to offer, as best we can, some solace and comfort..." My mind started to wonder as I began to think back about how things got to this point and how I came to be at this Memorial service.

The Memorial service was being held at the Washington DC Marine Barracks courtyard in honor of our fallen co-workers. The entire grounds were well guarded because of the number of very high-ranking officials in attendance, including the President. We had to RSVP if we were going to attend and we had to bring that RSVP with us to gain entrance to the ceremony. Since we would not be allowed to drive onto the Marine Barracks grounds, we had a choice of parking in the Maritime Plaza parking lot or the Navy Yard—both located some distance from the Marine Barracks. Buses were scheduled to transport us from the parking areas to the Marine Barracks.

I really wanted to attend the Memorial services because I lost friends and wanted to honor their memory. Since I wasn't sure I could drive past the Navy Yard, Shellie, our new Human Resources Director, offered to give me a ride. We arranged to meet on the upper deck of the Pentagon City Mall parking garage so she could pick me up. That way I didn't have to worry about driving near the Navy Yard in my upset condition. Having heard that the shooter killed friends and acquaintances, and after working with the 911 operator to provide locations of the shooter for the police, the stress was oppressive. Shellie was a great help in volunteering to drive near the Navy Yard.

Shellie asked if I wanted to park in the Maritime Plaza parking lot, and, of course I said yes. I was not ready to go back onto the Navy Yard right now. I knew there were other ways to get to the Maritime Plaza lot without having to drive onto the Navy Yard, even if they were more difficult. I could sense Shellie was getting ready to ask me if I'd rather go around to the Maritime lot in order to avoid the Navy Yard altogether, but I stopped that question before she could ask. It turned out that I was right about not being able to drive by the Navy Yard on my own. Instead, I asked her if we could just try driving past the Navy Yard. So, we drove past the Yard to see how I would handle the situation. I didn't take it well, but I did make it through with a minimum of tears. I asked if she minded turning around and driving past the yard again. She was so accommodating. She turned around and we drove by once again. I had the same reaction. Of course, now that we just left the Maritime Plaza, we had to return. So, Shellie turned her Jeep around and headed back past the Navy Yard one last time. That was enough for me right now. We parked and walked to the road outside where the buses were waiting.

When I boarded the bus, Wilma, my co-worker who ushered Jill into her office and hid with her under her desk, was already seated in the back, but came up to me and gave me a long hug. The tears rolled down my face. I was unashamed. Roland Kilgore, our finance department branch chair, came over after that and hugged me too. More tears. We have a few Roland's at NAVSEA so we usually identify him with his last name. That way, people immediately know which Roland we are talking about. Again, I cried unashamedly. Shellie held my hand. I don't know whether I cried because of our new normal, which wasn't even anything like a normal life at all, but was the best we could expect to be for a while; or because I had people who knew what I went through during the shooting ordeal.

When the bus was full, we departed to the barracks. The Marine barracks is only two blocks from the Navy Yard. The bus route had to skirt past the corner of the Yard on the way to the Marine Barracks. The bus ride was short; we easily could have walked the distance, but it was nice to have a little air conditioning, if even only for a few minutes. As we turned at the corner of the Yard, the bus traveled up the street and arrived at the barracks where we were dropped off on the sidewalk. Once again I started to cry. It was short-lived, but I had a hunch it was only the first of more tears that night. We were met by an escort and given directions to the entrance to the Marine Barracks. We then proceeded to the entrance way to the ceremony.

At the security gate, we had to place our personal effects on a table and then subject ourselves to a search. Passing through the metal detectors, we had to show our ID cards and produce our invitations. Luckily, all I brought with me were my wallet, book, and invitation. Since I didn't know what to expect and how long I would be waiting for the ceremony to begin, I had brought along a book to read. At this point I guess you could say I was in kind of a daze and just following the crowd. When the lady in front of me put her purse on the table, I did the same. I was not cognizant of what was going on around me. When I walked through the metal detector, I didn't realize I was being beckoned forward by the guard until I had already passed through. Then I realized he was looking up at the metal detector lights to see if I had any hidden metal on me. When I finished with security, I stepped aside to let Shellie, Wilma, and Wilma's escort come through the metal detector. While waiting on the other side of the barriers for the rest of my group, someone came up to us and offered bottles of water. I gratefully accepted one, knowing this would be a long event and there would be nowhere else to get something to drink until I got home.

We moved in toward the bleachers where I found a spot near the top so we would have a better view of the ceremony activities. We arrived at about 2:30 p.m. and people were still arriving at 5:00 p.m. when the ceremony was due to start. The Navy band played beautifully and made the solemn event a memorable one from the moment we entered the Marine Barracks grounds. Shellie sat with me, Wilma and her escort sat near us, and Lillian from the IT group sat in front of us, but I didn't even notice her until she turned around and introduced herself to me. Only then did I recognize her. Lillian and I had worked on a year-long project together and just finished recently, trying to get a legal program that scans CAC cards as acknowledgement of attendance for training. When the band began playing Amazing Grace, I lost it and started crying. I couldn't contain myself. It was an extremely emotional time for me. I was fortunate Shellie was there for me making sure I was OK. Even Wilma, who had been through so much more than me seemed to be doing much better. I only wished I was doing as well as her.

Then I saw one of the women who had been wounded by the shooter. She was here at the Memorial services, even after having undergone several surgeries on her injured shoulder in the past few days. She was the only wounded person I saw at the services. My heart just tore up for her. I cried again. After seeing her, I found myself ruminating over the terrible events that occurred just days prior. Again and again I was inexplicably drawn back to the moment I heard that when she was being assisted down the stairs by a group of her co-workers the shooter opened fire into the group and hit her in the shoulder. Then I got to contemplating about what Lillian told me about one of the men in her department. He was the facilities guy who pulled up the cubicle divider in front of his desk and threw it at the shooter in an attempt to stop him. The shooter fired his weapon through the divider and hit the man, instantly killing him. This brought back memories of my employee being shot at, and here I was crying again. I just couldn't help it. I can't even begin to imagine such bravery, and yet I thought about how the shooter continued to roam about the hallways killing more people unlucky enough to be caught in the wrong place at the wrong time. I switched between crying and frustration; anger, and more frustration. Then there was more crying.

My emotions began welling up inside me as I thought about being on the phone telling the 911 operator which directions I heard the shots coming from and how this seemed to do no good. It appeared to me even as I was telling the operator where the shots were coming from, that it was only hindering things because I just knew more people kept getting killed as I heard more shots being fired. The location of the shooter wasn't getting to the police fast enough. The shooter knew his way around Building 197; he knew his way around the girders, and he knew where to hide. The police were new to this building and didn't know how the girders came down at an angle from the ceiling in such a way as to be an optimal hiding place, and somewhere a spry person could get into and out of easily. To this day, I still feel it would have been better had I gone out into the hallway to make visual contact with the shooter so I could be more accurate in my reporting.

My thoughts were interrupted by applause accorded several military speakers who spoke of our fallen comrades. To me, they hit the mark when they spoke of those who were the epitome of honor, courage, and love of family and life. My emotions spiraled out of control! These were the heroes, the people who tried to shield others, tried to find out what was going on, even tried to stop the shooter. They were being honored and my heart went out to them, their familes, and the speakers' kind and noble words. The Secretaries of Defense and Navy; even the Deputy Secretary of Defense spoke of the people; their love of family and life and their contributions to NAVSEA and the Navy. The statements from these representatives were poignant; and heartwarming. I was so glad I came, I was bursting with pride for our fallen heroes and what they tried to do, and for those who helped them.

Then it was President Obama's turn to speak. He mentioned the names of the fallen and mentioned something personal about each individual. All in all a nice touch for the affected families and co-workers. Though he honored the fallen, he also used this event to push for gun control. His use of this forum to push his political agenda on gun control was very disheartening. I cried again, but for a different reason this time. I remember thinking that for someone to take the focus of this Memorial service away from the fallen and change it into a platform to shove a political agenda at us was unconscionable at best and worst case, totally unacceptable. I felt angry because I had higher expectations of a Commander and Chief. More tears. Even to this day I think back with shame that the President of the United States would stoop so low as to perpetrate such a brazen act of political philandering at this event. I cried some more. We lost our friends and co-workers to a crazy man for whom the system failed. Gun control wasn't the issue and wasn't going to bring the fallen back. The entire fiasco at the Navy Yard, in my opinion, was a direct result of multiple system failures at different government levels. I was thinking, "How dare he insult us like this and take away the honor due our fallen co-workers in order to push such a disingenuous and shameless agenda." His failure to recognize there were systemic failures was also appalling. Washington DCs Mayor Gray also got up, paid a little less due to the fallen and went almost directly into his political agenda for gun control. I expected as much of him. He has no civility in him and cares only for what he wants to accomplish while in office. I expect more of our President. I was relieved after the ceremony to find out I wasn't the only one in attendance who was insensed by the President's impertinent words. Other than those two affronts to our sensibilities, we all felt the fallen had been honored appropriately. I will miss them.[8]

Our old building remains a crime scene, and the authorities are still looking for lost bullets. Some of our personal effects are still being removed from the second floor and from the fifth floor as individual crime scenes are cleared. I understand the area I worked in will be one of the last to be cleared since it was the most heavily involved area and

---

[8] "So these families have endured a shattering tragedy. It ought to be a shock to us all as a nation and as a people. It ought to obsess us. It ought to lead to some sort of transformation. That's what happened in other countries when they experienced similar tragedies. In the United Kingdom, in Australia, when just a single mass shooting occurred in those countries, they understood that there was nothing ordinary about this kind of carnage. They endured great heartbreak, but they also mobilized and they changed, and mass shootings became a great rarity." Obama

"No other advanced nation endures this kind of violence -- none. Here in America, the murder rate is three times what it is in other developed nations. The murder rate with guns is ten times what it is in other developed nations. And there is nothing inevitable about it. It comes about because of decisions we make or fail to make. And it falls upon us to make it different." Obama

will take the longest to clear. We have been warned to try to make do with what we have if at all possible. Our personal effects will stay on our desks until the crime scene has been cleared, and after the repairs have been completed. Considering what I saw as I was being led out of the building during the height of the shooting, the shotgun shells would be the easiest part of the cleanup, but only after recreating the steps taken by the shooter. Repairing cubicles that had been shot into and the glass that was shattered must be done prior to anyone entering the area again. I don't think there is much to be gleened by anyone who hasn't seen the shattered glass and torn up cubicles to see them after the fact.

After the Memorial service, we boarded the buses and were taken back to the Maritime Plaza parking lot. However, there was little chance of getting out of the parking lot any time soon. Shellie and I sat in her Jeep waiting for about 15 minutes and never moved. Now, Shellie really had to use the Lady's room. It seems like she needed to use the facilities since before the Memorial service started. Now I also have the urge to use the restroom. This would be the perfect time to take a break from a very long afternoon and have a light meal too. Neither one of us ate before we left home around 1:00 p.m. A short bathroom break and a small bite to eat while waiting for the traffic to clear would also be good right about now. I suggested we park the car and walk to a nearby restaurant up Eigth Street about five blocks away. I offered to treat since Shellie picked me up and brought me to the Memorial service and then drove me in front of the Navy Yard several times on my first foray past the Yard since the shooting.

Shellie parked the car and we took a walk. We passed many questionable eateries before coming upon one that looked more suitable for sitting down to have a light repast. When we were seated, Shellie left for the restroom while our drinks were coming. I scanned the menu to see what my choices were. I couldn't make up my mind among three selections. When Shellie returned, the waitress came back to get our orders. My choices were narrowed to one when I was told the restaurant had no cream-based sauces. So, I had the Ahi Tartar. Shellie chose a hamburger. When the food came, we discussed the anger I felt at the two speakers who advanced their political agendas at the expense of the fallen victims. We both recognized the futility of that exercise, but I noted that it felt good to get the frustration out in the open. I then spoke of my upcoming trip to Texas to attend our granddaughter's fifth birthday. I just couldn't believe it had been five years since her dad returned from Iraq just in time for her birth. He just barely made it in time. We didn't spend long eating because we knew there would be a long drive ahead of us, so we headed right back to the parking lot as soon as we paid the bill for our dinners.

On the drive home Shellie drove me slowly past the Navy Yard one last time for me to see if I could do it without the tears. I quickly realized it would take many more trips before I could drive onto the Navy Yard. As we left the entrance way to the Navy Yard, I mentioned seeing one of the wounded survivors at the Memorial service. I said that as far as I could determine, she was the only wounded victim to have attended. I also noted how when she was wheeled off the field her face showed a level of discomfort that conveyed to me the state of her recovery. She didn't have to say a word, her expression said it all.[9]

An email received shortly after the Memorial service informed us the entire event was planned in 48 hours. We were also told it usually takes two weeks to plan for an event to which the President is invited.

---

[9] As reported on September 16, 2013, there were 13 fatalities. The suspect and 11 of the victims were killed at the scene, while a 13th victim, who was shot in the head, died at George Washington University Hospital. *All the victims killed were civilian employees or contractors. Eight others were injured, three of them from gunfire. The survivors wounded by gunshots (one police officer and two female civilians) were in critical condition at Washington Hospital Center.

It was hastily planned to show the country our leaders don't just take their time to recognize the fallen. They recognize the sacrifices of our dead, what types of people they were, some of the heroic actions that occurred, and what we, as an agency, went through. I felt a little less frustrated when I read the message. It meant the President rearranged his schedule to recognize our fallen. I was impressed.

There were 12 fatalities and 8 injuries. We honored those who lost their lives in the shooting at the Memorial Service. They were:

1. Michael Arnold, age 59
2. Martin Bodrog, age 53
3. Arthur Daniels, age 51
4. Sylvia Frasier, age 53
5. Kathy Gaarde, age 62
6. John Roger Johnson, age 73
7. Mary Francis Knight, age 51
8. Frank Kohler, age 50
9. Vishnu Pandit, age 61
10. Kenneth Bernard Proctor, age 46
11. Gerald Read, age 58
12. Richard Michael Ridgell, age 52

CHAPTER 12

A Caring Program

I opened my email the day after the Memorial Service and found a message from Shellie, our new Human Resources Director. She must have composed it after she got home from the service. She covered everything a great supervisor should to let subordinates know she cares for them and their recovery. When I read it I felt like she sent that email out for me. I knew she was writing the words for the others who were affected by the shooting, but it seemed like almost every item she discussed would be something I could use in my healing. As I read each item, the meaning resonated deeply inside me. Since her words had such a profound effect on me I feel it only proper they be included here. I can do no better than her in conveying her words. So, I'm giving you the body of her email with her paragraphs in quotes so you can see for yourselves how thoughtful she is, and I'll add my thoughts between her quoted paragraphs.

"On Monday morning, 16 September 2013, a violent attack in our workplace in Building 197 at the Washington Navy Yard has hurt us all. Our work lives, our sense of safety and security and, for some, our personal lives have been altered. Many of our coworkers, family members and friends have experienced great fear and anxiety worrying for our safety as news of the attack's events unfolded. Now, we endeavor to recover."

This is the first paragraph of the email that was delivered to us from our new HR Director, who is still acclimating herself to the unique culture of NAVSEA. It was delivered the day after she observed our unique NAVSEA family, members of different directorates, hugging each other, and holding hands as we cried together. It was comforting to know that our chain of command cared enough to begin sorting out the event in an attempt to begin the healing process. Until she saw us interacting, I'm not sure she knew how many people we worked with in other directorates, and I'm not sure she knew how much we were affected by the loss of fellow friends and coworkers.

"As your Director of Civilian Human Resources, I want to assure each of you in SEA 10H that you and your family's well-being is the top priority as we rebuild."[10] "I have asked each supervisor to ensure each of you is helped in your return to work and to provide you with care and support as we all recover. Please let your supervisors know if you suffered an injury or illness; if you experienced the attack, and let your supervisor know if you or your family needs help. Supervisors will keep me informed of everyone's progress so I can ensure that support and help is provided where and when needed."

During the first week after the shooting, I thought I could shake the feelings I had; the guilt, the fear, the anxiety, anguish, all of it. But as I jumped awake each hour during the night, I found I couldn't heal myself. I made use of the crisis line. It's been a little over a week now. When I spoke to Nina, I found not only was she not back at work, but she was seeing a therapist and psychiatrist. The crisis center set up an emergency appointment for me with a psychiatrist at Walter Reed on

---

[10] SEA 10H is a Directorate within NAVSEA Headquarters. The Headquarters has many branches, each with its own code; for example, Workforce Development is SEA10H5, and no other branch is recognized by the number 5 in their code.

a temporary basis. CEAP found a therapist in the city where I live. As an addendum; six weeks later, I was still seeing both and not doing that much better, except for my sleep. Three months had gone by at this time in my writing, and I still need help. I thought I was strong enough to take care of my own healing, but I found out differently.

Back to the HR Director's email; she went on to state, "We need each other now more than ever. The SEA 10H staff I have come to know is strong, caring and supportive. We will establish a SEA 10H volunteer team of Buddy Shipmates as a source of in-house help and support to all members of SEA 10H and our contractor comrades."

Shellie's email let me know it was OK to not be OK, and it was OK to ask for help. The underlying message of the HR Director may have been asking us what kind of person we were; whether we were the kind of person who could remain strong in light of the shooting incident, or were in need of assistance to help deal with any resulting emotional disorders.

In her email appeal to begin the Buddy Shipmates program, the Director further asked, "If you would like to volunteer to be a Buddy Shipmate, I ask that you complete the information in the attached SEA 10H Shipmate Buddy Commitment Profile and return it to my point of contact in the SEA10H3 Labor and Employee Relations Branch using the contact information provided in my note. My appointed lead will publish a roster of volunteer Shipmate Buddies. Those who would like to have a Shipmate Buddy should make contact with this office so the connections and commitments can be made."

It was comforting to know that professional counseling and assistance were being made available on a 24/7 basis to all SEA 10H staff and family/household members. The HR Director noted that SEA 10H staff were, "Covered by the Federal Occupational Health's Civilian Employee Assistance Program (CEAP)." She asked that we keep a wallet-sized CEAP card with us and to ensure our dependent family members and any household members understand they are also covered by CEAP for support and assistance. To its credit, the Navy made CEAP professional counselors available every day, all week long, and intended to continue making them availabale for the next year. The Director went on to reiterate, "Please do not hesitate to call a CEAP counselor at the phone numbers provided on the CEAP card or go on-line at the website also indicated on the card using your password and user ID."

She continued, "We were made aware of the following important helpful points about violent incidents in the workplace, which originated from the Department of Labor, Occupational Health and Safety Administration (OSHA).

a. Witnessing or experiencing workplace violence is traumatic and can affect individuals physically, emotionally and psychologically.
b. The usual response to sudden and potentially life-threatening situations is at first to feel surprised or stunned, and then to feel extremely fearful, followed by a sense of anger as you attempt to respond to the crisis.
c. During traumatic events, your heart rate increases and your blood pressure elevates, muscles may tighten to prepare for escape, and your attention and concentration are focused on finding a way to survive.
d. After a violent workplace incident, reactions to trauma can continue to be experienced anywhere from a few hours or days to a month. Victims may experience sleeplessness, excessive alertness and repeated memories of the event. It is also common to withdraw from others and prefer to be alone in a quiet place."

She wanted us to know she realized where many of us were in our progress toward healing and she understood we weren't far along that path. Her understanding statements were like a breath of fresh air to me; just to read this email gave me encouragement that someone in my chain of command recognized that we all needed time to heal.

   e. Shellie continued in more depth with her knowledge of what trauma can do to some people by saying, "In addition to actual physical injuries, victims of workplace violence may experience:
- (1) short- and long-term psychological trauma;
- (2) fear of returning to work;
- (3) changes in relationships with coworkers and family;
- (4) feelings of incompetence, guilt or powerlessness; and/or,
- (5) fear of criticism by leaders or supervisors."

Her words put forth such a feeling of caring I felt encouraged about being accepted by others and cared for by her. I didn't even really know her because she was not my immediate supervisor, and yet I felt like she knew me by what she said in her email. Even though her email was sent to the entire HR staff, I felt like she was being informative and letting just me know she realized I was hurting.

On the basis of these important notes, we were asked by the Director to, "Please reach out and ask for help or support as early as possible if you or a coworker experience troubling emotional symptoms associated with the Building 197 trauma. Please know that several types of assistance are readily available to help each of us through any post-incident problems and to help identify symptoms to address them as early as possible. We are a team, we are a family. Your well-being, and that of your family, is top priority. Thanks to everyone for helping each other."

This woman has insight and appeared to me to be a very caring individual. All it took was for her to see how we interacted and cared for each other at the Memorial, even when we weren't in the same directorate to know we were a close family. She perceived that insight from interacting with us, and seeing us interact with each other. Of course, every time she heard me sob, she turned to see if I was going to be all right. Even between the tears, when the speeches were about a speaker's agenda, she would turn around to check on me, making sure I was okay. Very few people have the aptitude to put into words the caring message she put forth, and very few people would put those caring insights into words. More than that, many in leadership positions would worry more about themselves and what would happen to them if work stopped or slowed than about those who were so affected by that terrible day that they couldn't work. Here was a woman who was talking about us getting help and helping each other. The focus wasn't about getting our work done or deadlines. The emphasis was on our healing. She saw us suffering and put her words to us solely about healing. Of course, part of her insight may have been what she was seeing in me or us all, and part may have been in how she saw us all suffer. It doesn't really matter how she got that insight, but rather that she had it.

I think the fact that we in SEA10H were so affected by the loss we suffered, and didn't mind showing our feelings, that the HR Director couldn't help but be affected in the same way. When you are around dozens of people in the stands during a memorial service, and they are openly crying, there is no way one cannot be affected. Our HR Director walked out of there as silently as we did, and surely felt the same emotions we did. Otherwise, she wouldn't, couldn't have written that email with such a caring "voice." Even though the shooting started near us and affected us and the IT sections the most, Shellie is located a floor below us and at the far end of the hallway and is responsible for us, our work, and our well being. She feels the loss of co-workers, friends, and continuity as much as we do, and it hurts.

I did not avail myself of the "Shipmate Buddy" program. It never materialized. I'm not sure what happened to make the program not become a full fledged program. I don't believe the ongoing sequester affected the program because the manpower would have been voluntary. Importantly, I feel it would have been helpful to those of us who desperately wanted to get back to work to have someone to turn to when needed. Three months later, the program still has not begun. If it did, I would have asked for a buddy. Once I was fully acclimated, I would most assuaradly have volunteered to be a buddy, knowing I would be able to help someone else assimilate back into the NAVSEA family. If I was "king for a day," I would implement the program, call for voluinteers, and if I had none, I'd do what leadership usually does, assign volunteers to be in the program to help those in need.

The closest I've come to having a buddy is my supervisor, who volunteers to walk with me when the tears, the inevitable tears appear. There were times when she wasn't there and times when she was. During some walks I cried alone and some she accompanied me, when we cried together. Eventually the tears subsided and the sobs turned into teary eyed walks, which suited me just fine. I expect that someday soon, those tears will go away, and I'll return to normal. I look forward to that day. Counseling is still available and will be for a year. If I need it I know I can always avail myself of the counseling that is available. The lack of the buddy system was a blow to me when I found it wasn't implemented.

Assistance from peers would be a more natural method to talk about fears and demons that still haunt me when least expected. It is a shame this program didn't get off the ground. In spite of this fact, I survived the shooting at the Navy Yard and am working hard to survive the aftermath visits of demons and sudden onslaught of fears that occur almost regularly, until I reach a normal state. By normal, I mean the old normal, not the "new normal" that I am experiencing right now. This new normal is only temporary and is NOT going to be me forever.

As it is, I've had to cope with the aftermath of the shooting in a different manner. Prescription medications help me temporarily keep the demons at bay during the night time hours, and help me get to sleep. There is nothing that helps during the day. I suffer constant flashbacks during the day.

Though we don't have the buddy system, I've become a buddy to my early arriving employee. She isn't quite ready to come back to work, but has come to the new building we're using while the old one is being repaired. She came to the Christmas party and spent almost the entire day there. I warned her that she would fall asleep that night before her son because the first day back at work would wear her out if she didn't leave right after the party but she didn't leave. She told me just before she left that she was worn out. I provided some hints about how she might work through her evening with her young son so she could get away with falling asleep on the couch while they were watching TV, and warned her again that she would definitely fall asleep. I told her my story about how I fell asleep early in the evening after my first day back as an example, and continued to fall asleep early for several more weeks until I had become acclimated to the work world again. I also suggested that if she wanted to try coming back to work, she initially try coming back on a part time basis because she'll tire easily. She was grateful for the help and left right after our discussion to start her evening activities. It was good therapy for me too, to be able to let someone know about the strain that occurs when coming back to work after being away for so long.

Time has passed. It's been four months since I've been back at work and I feel myself becoming a little stronger every day. I still become so engrossed in my work that I tune out most everything around me. This makes me appear flighty and forgetful. I have to work on becoming more aware of what is going on around me. I find people have to ask me questions twice before I'm even aware they are standing at my cubicle waiting for a reply from me. Other than that, I am becoming more independent every day and am working toward becoming better at seeing what lies ahead. There are still areas of myself and my psyche that need some tender loving care, but I can take care of them by not pushing myself too hard. I am better off just taking my healing process one day at a time.

There are times when I can make a decision immediately, but other times when I am totally indecisive and just can't make make up my mind. A condition I'm sure - that will end at some point in the future. But, not tomorrow or the next day, or even next week, or next month. I think there is a possibility of it ending sometime in the coming months. By then I'll be able to make decisions about issues that come my way. For right now, decisiveness eludes me.

Right after the shooting incident, I didn't realize the true extent to which I was affected emotionally. It took about a week to make the connection between the events of the shooting and my mental condition. I found help and am receiving help for my emotional needs. I know now this help is something I'll be needing for quite a while in order to follow the path of returning to normal.

Now that I've had time to reflect on the events of that terrible day, and know how they so drastically affected me, if I had to do it all over again I might find myself reacting differently. I may not have called 911, or if I forgot myself and dialed it automatically, I might not have stayed on the phone. I would most likely have run out and kept going out the front gate. I wouldn't be spending two days a week in some doctor or therapist's office trying to get my life back in order again. But, and here comes the indecisiveness again, then again, maybe I would still dial 911 and stay on the line with them. I just can't seem to stay out of the way when an action needs to be taken. However, I would have stepped out of my cubicle to get a better look at where the shooter was heading after he left my area so I could give an "eyeball" location to the operator. It would most likely have helped me to know where Nina went when she ran out of my cubicle and I wouldn't have been so worried about her for so long.

Though I would rather not have gone through this event at all, I feel that the experience has made me more aware of what others who have gone through a traumatic event similar to this would be feeling and some insight into how they are coping and adjusting to the changes the experience caused in their lives. I was one of the lucky ones. I was not in the wrong place at the wrong time. I was in a situation where I was able to call 911 and provide assistance for well over 45 minutes. Although I lament my situation as I think about it, I could have been in a much worse situation. I shouldn't complain. I should be grateful that I'm alive and able to tell this story.

Thinking back to to the aftermath of the shooting, one item keeps popping into my head. It occurred to me that when I safely reached a sanctuary building, I spent all of my time looking for my supervisor, co-worker and employee, desperate to find out if they were even alive. This drained me, but I didn't realize it until the following day. My focus was on mustering my people and finding them alive. If I'd found they were killed in the shooting, I don't know how I would have handled that situation. I used to think I would know what I'd do. Now I'm not so sure.

I've gone through many life-changes over my 60 plus years; however, over the last several months it seems as though I've experienced as much emotional turmoil as in my previous 30 years in the workforce. That's a lot of changes to have to deal with in such a short time. Am I the person I thought I would be coming out of this situation? That's hard to say. Today, I would say yes. I would say I'm master of my domain. Tomorrow might be a rough day, and I would say no. I would say I'm consigned to drift in the wind in whichever direction it takes me. I did find out I'm obedient, when I listened to the 911 operator and didn't leave my hiding place to look around. As a matter of fact, I'm probably too obedient. Perhaps that coincides with the part of me that is indecisive on the rough days and needs to be told what to do, lest I go in a direction different from what my boss would like. If this is my character, was it always there? Would I always pick up the phone and call 911 in an emergency because it had been drilled into me all these years? Was this just one instance of calling to get police there fast or was it just this one time?

Thinking back to a situation that occurred in Rockville, MD when I was walking to the Metro station, I saw a bus with the rolling sign across the front that said, "EMERGENCY, CALL POLICE" instead of the usual destination. I pulled out my cell phone and dialed 911 to let them know the bus location and what the placard said. Adding that information to the Navy Yard incident, I have to say I would always call 911, even though it may end up the same way, with me in therapy. Hearing what I heard, the shooter saying, "Fourth floor, then something mumbled," then a shot, knowing someone was being shot, and most likely killed, has profoundly affected me. I know it will take some time to heal. I'll always wonder if I should have picked up a chair and shoved it into the shooter from behind, or even just rushed him from behind. But I digress.

The HR Director continues on with her message, encouraging us to help each other:

"Please reach out and ask for help or support as early as possible if you or a coworker experience troubling emotional symptoms associated with the Building 197 trauma."

"Please know that several types of assistance are readily available to help each of us through any post-incident problems and to help identify symptoms to address them as early as possible."

"We are a team, we are a family. Your well-being, and that of your family, is top priority. Thanks to everyone for helping each other."

This insightfuil woman appears to be a very caring individual. I like her and I haven't even worked with her yet. I look forward to working with her when I am able to return to work. She shows great insight and understanding.

After all, what other new person on board would come and meet me to take me to the Memorial Service, and drive me past the Navy Yard several times to help me get over that hurdle. She didn't have to do that, and she certainly didn't have to come all the way down to the mall to meet me just to drive me back up to the DC area for the Service. She sat next to me at the Service and turned to make sure I was all right several times during the Service when she heard the sobs. She has an uncanny ability to sense when someone needs her and she knew I needed her at that point in time.

Even our leadership let us know in a short email that we should take time to heal, but this new Director said it in the right way, and even backed up her words with actions.

My boss, who saw the shooter, and was I'm sure, as traumatized as I, traveled to my home to make sure I was OK. Even though her visit was cut short when I received the phone call informing me of an immediate appointmeint with a psychiatrist, she helped me get ready so I could get there on time.

I have to admit, Shellie is an impressive person. I know her workload just expanded now that this shooting incident is displacing the people she is responsible for to different buildings. That will affect the methods for how she conducts meetings, or how many meetings she can conduct. I imagine now more and more meetings will be electronic or telephonic to save time and reduce inconvenience.

As I think back on the shooting and how I attempted to reconcile the incidents that occured that day, I find it reasonable to be able to extract some lessons learned from my experience.

Of primary importance to me was the number of employees in Building 197 who were physically and emotionally traumatized as a result of the shooting situation that occurred on September 16, 2013. This trauma has, or is making it extremely difficult for some individuals to once again become effective team members in a non-threatening and productive work environment at the Navy Yard. The Situation was that of being placed in unexpected danger from a shooter who managed to get past security. The result manifested itself in overly stressed and emotionally disturbed survivors.

One of the earliest tasks of the FBI and Department of Labor was to provide counselors for emotional support and physical oversight on the first day. For team members requesting assistance in the recovery and reasimilation process at work, the government provided follow-on assistance in the form of CEAP, which would be made available for a year. The suggestion of the Buddy Shipmate system by Shellie also was an excellent suggestion that would provide internal, direct help to survivors.

In response to her suggestion, the HR Director/NAVSEA attempted to put into place a program of Shipmate Buddies to provide responsive, one-on-one real-time emotional and physical support to help individuals deal with the stress of readjusting to their new workplace environment. From my experience, this solution did not fully materialize.

I have no doubt that if the Shipmate Buddy program was implemented fully, it would have worked. Since the Shipmate Buddy program was not implemented, what worked for me was the ability to take breaks when needed so I could go outside when I had to cry. Another aspect that worked well for me was my psychiatrist's treatment plan of going back to work on a two to three day a work week schedule, and then adding a fourth day and eventually a fifth day after gettting used to the workplace again.

As a means of assisting the families of the victims toward healing, NAVSEA opened Building 197 to the families so they could see the places where their loved ones worked. Of course the building was cleaned up. All the blood was removed from the shooting sites so as to make the family members more at ease with viewing the office spaces. Once family members were allowed into Building 197, survivors began asking why they were not allowed to visit the building to continue their healing process. NAVSEA leadership made the decision to allow the survivors to begin entering the building. I must say my entrance into the building allowed me to see the same area the shooter was seeing when he was standing behind me for such a long time. I still fail to see what he was standing there so long for. All that was visible was the opposite and sides of the fourth and fifth floors, but nothing from there down to the first floor. One would think a better view would be desired by someone who was looking for a vantage point.

Seeing the third floor room where the shooter was killed was redeeming to me. Though most of the panels in the cubicles were removed, along with the glass, I could see the dents in the metal of the drop ceiling and where the projectiles hit the metal frame around the doors. I continue my recovery; continue with therapy, seeing the psychiatrist, and talking with others who have gone through this ordeal. While months later I'm still in the healing process, I can say I feel a little better every day. Therefore, I believe CEAP has helped me, as has the crisis center when I needed it most. Sadly, the Shipmate Buddy system is not a working system, and so is not working for me. I would suggest that the program get started and, once started, allow us to join in. When we get better, we'll be able to join the Shipmate Buddy system as a Buddy and help others who still need the program to return to normal as we used to know it.

My forward movement plateaued after I'd gone to the five day workweek. For some reason I was having trouble making any progress. Even though I started the EMDR sessions, I truly had only started them so couldn't say they were yet working. My Mind and Body sessions would help if I could concentrate enough to start my grounding technique. When I discussed this problem with my psychiatrist, she recommended returning to the four day work week and starting from there again. However, when I mentioned that not only my supervisor, but everyone else in the branch was engaged with the shooting in some manner, she changed her recommendation to have me moved out of that section to one that was not so closely involved with the shooter. I now work semi-independently with a different supervisor and second rater on a new and interesting set of programs. Though I'm still learning them and am picking up more programs to work, I am moving forward now in the healing process. I have found, though, that the healing process is a slow one. While the Shipmate Buddy System never did catch hold, I'm not sure that would have helped as much as moving to a peaceful and quiet environment. The people in the new area do offer assistance whenever they find I need it for my phobias, and I don't hesitate to take them up on their offers. So, even though the Shipmate Buddy System isn't in effect, we have our own Buddy System in a quieter area where I am completing my healing process.

As I look back on that fateful day, I am grateful fate put us survivors in the places we were that morning. Some would say those who died were in the wrong place at the wrong time, and that may have saved some lives. Others would say the survivors had a life altering experience they will forever remember. I have noticed that in life-threatening situations and their aftermaths, some people have come to realize who they really are and who they have really become. I now realize how important family is, and have been devoting more of my time to family than I did before. People who weren't as affected by this event as those of us on the fourth floor may not have changed much in their view of life. It depends on the person, or should I say, the make up of the person, how much the shooting has changed each individual, and the views of each individual toward life and family.

CHAPTER 13

Treatment Trials

I woke with a start. What woke me was the part of a nightmare where I begin falling to my death. In this nightmare, I am hiding in my cubicle and feel the footfalls of the shooter coming around the end of my cubicle. He'd just run up the stairs, slamming the stairwell fire safety door open, after shooting someone on a floor below. He was crouching while holding his shotgun ready to shoot someone if they came out of their cubicles on this deserted floor.

In my dream, when I heard the stairwell door slam, I would come out from my hiding place, and when I felt those footfalls on the flooring, I moved in a crouch toward the front side of my cubicle doorway. As the barrell of the shotgun began to show, I moved slowly toward the doorway with my hands up at a slight angle and reaching for the shotgun barrel. As I saw the shooter's shoes come into sight, I ran at him in this same pose. One hand grabbed the barrel and the other continued to push against him as my body's weight added power behind that arm. The surprise put the shooter off his stance. We kept going into the cubicle across from mine, and against the counter of that cubicle. He recovered and pushed back. I regrabbed the barrel of the shotgun so he couldn't swing it around and shoot me, and then swung it using it to move his forward momentum even harder toward the hallway between the cubicles knowing he wouldn't let go of his deathgrip on his weapon. He and I both ended up in the hallway and I continued pushing him as he bounced off of my cubicle wall and into me. That pushed us both forward at an angle toward the balcony still struggling with the weapon. Finally, we were headed directly toward the balcony and I pushed harder as the shooter struggled to both push back at me and free his weapon at the same time.

Before he knew it, his back was at the balcony and I was pushing him over as he grabbed the balcony rail in an attempt to not go over. He grabbed me instead and we both went over. He had his shotgun in one hand and me in the other, as we both fell to our deaths on the floor below. These reccurring nightmares are what led me to see a psychiatrist. He prescribed sleeping pills, and boy, was I ready and willing to try them! The first night, the pill worked and I went to sleep. The second night was totally different. It didn't work and I shivered my way through the night until just before dawn when I must have nodded off. I was disappointed, but didn't give up. I took the sleeping pills again the third night. I went to sleep just fine, but when I got up to use the bathroom and decided to get a drink of water it wasn't the same. I climbed back into bed and just lay there for a while wondering if this was going to be a repeat of the previous night. The next thing I knew, I was opening my eyes to daylight.

It worked! I thought it wouldn't work when I wandered around the house and went to the kitchen to get some water; but the sleeping pills worked! I was so encouraged I just couldn't believe it! The success of those two nights; the first and third nights, was an indication to me that there was hope for a full night's sleep, and on a regular basis, too. I should have gone for help sooner! OK, I'd made it through the night. Things were looking up. I felt great after a full night's rest. I hadn't had a full night's rest since the day before the shooting. I began to look forward to tonight. After a day of trying to concentrate, paying bills, writing receipts into my checkbook, doing a little shopping for things we needed, cooking a couple of meals, the shadows were growing longer, and evening was quickly approaching. I barely made it outside to check on my garden before it got dark. I still hadn't finished all the things that were on my to-do list, but I did make a little dent in it.

After a few moments of settling down after a hectic day of chores, it was time to take that sleeping pill. I was looking forward to another good night's sleep. Tonight was different though. I didn't go to sleep right away, and when I finally got to sleep, I certainly didn't stay asleep. As I lie there waiting for sleep to arrive, I wondered what I'd done differently this day than I did yesterday or the day before. The answer escaped me and still does. I finally got up to check my email. After all, when I was emailing the kids yesterday, I was falling asleep in the middle of two sentences; in the middle of a two sentence email, doggone it! And here I was writing answers to emails by the paragraphs and am unable to drop off to sleep.

After an hour of answering emails, I went back to bed thinking I was just missing something, but that wasn't the case. Again, I just lay there. I began to play games in my mind about the "sleep fairy" traveling up from my feet. Even that didn't work, so I got up again. I spent another hour on email and then another hour in bed. After a few more hours of this I was thinking I might as well stay up. I almost did. I finally broke down and drank some wine. When that didn't help, I called the crisis hot line.

I poured my heart out to the poor counselor on the other end of the line; I felt better. He was a gem. At no time did he get impatient with my blubbering. Finally, I had one more drink and loaded it with good ole American Honey whiskey. Mind you, this is at 0500 and I should be getting up in a couple of hours, but I wanted to get at least a couple hours of sleep. I did get a little over one hour, from six-something to nearly quarter to eight.

This would prove to be a rough day. I checked my email. Again, I would miss the SEA10 telecon. I had to cook up a little something to eat and then head off to my appointment at Walter Reed Hospital. I needed to let my psychiatrist know about last night. Actually, he needed to know about the success of the first few nights and the dismal failure of last night. I needed to know what went wrong so I knew what not to do tonight. I'm not sure I ever want to go through a night like that again. When the medication didn't work, all the tricks I knew to use to help me get to sleep (nevermind staying asleep) didn't work. To me, the fear of having my nightmare occurring as a "daymare" scared me. I would inadvertently begin thinking about that situation as my mind ran at unheard of speeds instead of settling down for a rest. The prospect of the nightmares turning into daymares was too scarey to think about, but there I was worried about how that very situation was going to affect me nightly and daily if I couldn't get a full night's sleep.

The doctor added another prescription medication to get me to fall asleep. He told me to start with 2mg and raise it by 2mg after a couple of days if that didn't work. We'd previously talked about my grandchildren and the doctor suggested we take some time to visit them. He also suggested visiting the grandchildren would help me along my path to healing from this trauma. I jumped at that suggestion. I would ask my husband immediately about planning a trip to see the grandkids as soon as possible. The additional medication gave me the hope of getting sleep again so taking a trip would be less scarey now. Now, I have a dilemma because since my appointment took so long and I was heading home in rush hour traffic, I would not make it to my counseling appointment in time. However, I not only forgot my cell phone at home when I left, I also left my counselor's phone number on my kitchen counter with the phone. These are great things to find out when you're running late and need to call to let your appointment know you will be a little late!

At the Walter Reed pharmacy, I turned in the prescription the doctor gave me and then ran down the hallway to where I used to work in Building 1. When I turned the corner there was a plastic sheet hanging from the ceiling and a sign hanging on it stating the hallway was closed for construction work. Sudden stop. What now? The hallway was blocked off. I turned in circles. Someone came out from the opposite hallway and saw me looking lost. He didn't even have to ask, but he started to. I asked where the old Naval Medical Manpower Training and Education (NMMPT&E) moved to and he said it was down the hallway he'd just come from. I asked if he could show me where one of my old friends' office was. He shocked me by telling me my friend didn't work there anymore and that he'd taken a job at the Bureau of Medicine (BUMED). Then I asked about another friend and he showed me where he worked, but the office was dark. Then I asked about the training aid and was told she moved somewhere else too. Gee, I never thought that when I took another job, everyone I knew in my older job would move away to new jobs.

Then I told him I was running late to my next appointment and needed to use a telephone. He not only let me use his phone, he helped me look up the main number to my counselor so I could let her know I couldn't make it to our session that day. I thanked him and told him why I was seeing a psychiatrist and counselor so he wouldn't think I was totally crazy. He was sympathetic and understood how I could end up with two appointments in one day, five hours apart, and still end up missing one of them. Having made my phone call, I could now go back to the pharmacy and pick up my prescriptions and head to the Pentagon to pick up some slugs so I could grab the HOV-3 lane on I-95 heading south and get home at a reasonable time.

I left the hospital and took I-495 south, taking the exit for the George Washington (GW) Parkway so I could cut off a few miles and save some time too. Trucks aren't allowed on The GW Parkway so there isn't a lot of passing that has to be done to keep up the speed limit. That road leads all the way to the I-395 South, and the Pentagon exits. The Pentagon is a major staging area for slug activity, both pick-up and drop-off. I got off at the Pentagon exit and headed to the south parking lot; the slug staging parking lot. Following the road all the way to the south parking lot takes me to the area where the cars pick up people (slugs) from the Pentagon who are headed south; I look for the bus area to get my bearings to be sure I'm headed in the right direction. The slug pick up/drop off area is near the bus staging area so that's how I get my bearings in such a large place.

For those not familiar with slugging, it's a term for a hitch hiker in the DC region; part of a legal hitch-hiking set-up arrangement located at various key spots around the DC area where people stand to wait for a ride to a commuter lot along the I-95 corridor from the Woodbridge Township to the city of Fredericksburg. Drivers pull up to the appropriate commuter lot sign, open their window and yell out how many they'll take and, in some cases, which commuter lot they are going to. Even though they pull up by a sign, they still need to state the commuter lot to avoid confusion because some of the signs contain the names of two commuter lots. Then the asked-for number of people from the front of the line get into the car and follow the driver's lead for silence or talking for the rest of the ride. There is even a set of rules posted on the web for slugging. Once at the appropriate lot, the driver stops at the bus shelter to let the slugs off and continues out of the lot and back on the road on the way to his or her home. Why is this done? Why, to be able to take the High Occupancy Vehical (HOV)-3 lane, of course; it saves about one-half to one hour of driving in stop-and-go traffic. The only thing I had to remember was to get off at the right exit so I wouldn't miss my turn to the correct parking lot for the slugs headed in my direction. Getting around the Pentagon parking lots to the right slug line can be a bit tricky. This was the first time I used the slug line at the Pentagon and I needed to learn where to go to pick up the slugs headed in my direction. I lucked out and found the right slug line after having to go around the parking lots only once. I grabbed my slugs and we pulled onto the road that led to the highway. There was just one more corner to turn to get there and that corner was under police direction. I started driving onto the highway with the radio on for the news but, my little car is so loud with the rumbling of the highway it wasn't any use. Since we couldn't hear the radio, I turned it off and we drove in silence. We waited for the police direction to turn onto the HOV-3 lanes and when he gave us the go-ahead, we were off!

When my appointments at Walter Reed go overtime, or I end up spending extra time waiting for perscriptions to be filled, picking up slugs allows me to take the HOV-3 lanes and travel just 20 minutes for 19 miles of the trip south until the HOV-3 ends and merges with the I-95 main line traffic. Since I typically save two-hours of commuting time by taking the HOV-3 lanes, the rest of the trip, though slower, still allows us to get to the commuter lot faster than had I gone without slugs. When we get to the commuter lot where the slugs have their cars, I drop them off and head home, still getting home earlier than I would have if I didn't pick up anyone.

When I got home I started getting supper ready and didn't even check my email. I did; however, check my voicemail. I had one call from my therapist about my rescheduled session. I called her back intending to leave a message. I couldn't believe she picked up the phone and answered it. I wasn't prepared for an answer and had my voicemail message composed in my head. Now I had to backtrack and talk to her. I blurted out my name and told her I didn't expect anyone to still be working at this time of night. I then asked if she received my voicemail. She said she did and asked if I was okay. I told her I was and explained the events of the day. She asked if I had gotten any medication to help me sleep. I replied that I had received additional medication from my doctor at Walter Reed. We set up a tentative appointment for 1:30 p.m. the next day. We only talked for about 15 minutes, but since dinner was on the stove, I checked everything to make sure I didn't burn it while busy on the phone.

That call done, I remembered hearing the beeps, signs that I had a voicemail. So, as long as my hands were clean, I went into the den to listen to my voice mail messages. One particular voicemail was from a person named Julie. She was with the Department of Labor and wanted to ask me some questions about the CA-1 form I filed, one of those Workman's Comp. forms I wrote about earlier. I copied her number and the list of items she wanted me to provide information about. I listened to the message three times to make sure I heard it right and got all the information she wanted and her phone number, plus her name. Then it was back to the kitchen to check on dinner. I wasn't about to start over with a new batch of veggies if I burned these, it was now 7:00 p.m. and just too late. Starting over would have us eating at 8:30. I grabbed the phone off the wall thinking I could leave her a voicemail so I didn't have to remember to call her tomorrow. That way she could listen to it when she got to the office in the morning. At least that way, I could answer some of her questions and let her know which ones I didn't understand so she could explain them to me when she returned my call.

"Hello." Again, silence. What's with these people? Don't they have a life? What are they doing at work at 7:00 p.m.? Moment of recovery; then I told her who I was and asked her what she was doing at the office so late? She told me she works from home. That explained it. My turn. I had to let her know why I didn't identify myself right away. I told her I just got home and listened to her voicemail so I was prepared to leave a voicemail to let her know I'd received it and would be calling back tomorrow. I also told her I didn't have the answers to all the questions she asked so we went over them together. She gave me a case file number and even told me who she thought my adjudicator would be. I thanked her and hung up.

Many questions hung in my head. Why does a shooting from a week ago still affect me like this? My dreaded laptop. Why does the sight of my work laptop still send chills down my spine with the memories of what I heard and saw that day? Why do I immediately go into fright mode when I look at that laptop, even when I know I'm in my safe house? What makes that happen just by looking at it? How is it that I could continue to work on it while still on the Navy Yard, but now I can't even look at it? Why couldn't I move it to the den from where I put it when I got home that fateful night? Why can't I even touch it? Why? Why our building? Why shoot those people? Today I don't have time to dwell on these questions, thank God. If I did, I'd end up with another sleepless night; no sleep and a walking zombie.

Dinner has several parts to it and all need attending at the same time. Cooking redirects my focus from all these memories and I'm grateful for the respite. I call my husband in and we eat together while finishing a crossword puzzle. Before the shooting my husband and I planned a trip to Texas to visit the grandkids. We discuss the trip to visit the grandkids after the crossword puzzle is complete. I'm not letting him forget that; after all, the doctor recommended it. Hubby is working on his tractor project in his workshop, and gives me the updated status of the work.

The rear tire guard on my husband's tractor was cracked when he backed into a tree branch while mowing. It always looked lopsided so he took on this little project. He built up the area by riveting some metal in place after having shaped it in the shape of the other back wheel cover. Then he fiberglassed it, sanded, and filled the little air holes and then sanded some more. The wheel guard looked great and now must be painted. He's afraid if he waits to paint until we come back from our trip to see the grandkids, it will be too cold to paint and with the way the weather has been lately, he may be right.

Our plans were to leave on our trip that Friday, but the tractor fender still needed to be painted, and returning to the painting after we returned might not be an option if the weather turned colder. This was the time of the year the seasons could change in no time at all and the colder weather would make painting out of the question until spring. I called the kids to find out if they would mind our visit holding off a day. The trip to Texas usually involves stopping halfway to stay with our daughter. They both said delay would be fine. Our son even thought that since the shooting, the trip was off. But both my psychiatrist and counselor thought that visiting the grand kids would be good therapy for me, especially now that I had two prescription drugs to help me get to sleep and then stay asleep.

I mentioned the laptop earlier and now I need to explain that dreaded laptop. I worked on that laptop on the day of the shooting, once settled in the sanctuary, until the battery ran out. I finished one project and was well on my way to completing another project. I managed to keep it with me through thick and thin that entire day and into the night. I brought it in with me when I finally got home. I put it on the dryer next to my bag in the laundry room. And that is where I left it. I never brought it back into my office. My husband brought it to my office for me and placed it on the daybed behind my desk. I haven't opened it. It still has a dead battery. I haven't touched it. I can't bring myself to touch it. My counselor has given me an assignment; to turn sideways in my chair and gently brush my hand across the top without looking at it. I'm working on it, but it isn't easy. My psychiatrist, temporary though he may be, says all things take time, and healing from this will take time too.

The week following the shooting, our group from work had a date planned to attend a tour of the Capitol building. Due to our new situation, we contemplated cancelling the trip. However, I suggested we continue as planned. It would give us a chance to get together again and do something other than think about the shooting. A special tour guide and special parking were arranged so we could get right into one of the buildings without delay. This would allow us to spend more time going through the Capitol. More than anything, we needed that tour now. We needed to be able to focus on something else and be together as a team again. Jill kept the schedule and also added a group therapy session afterward. It was wonderful seeing everyone again, and not being on the Navy Yard anywhere near where the shooting occurred. We all met at Joint Base Anacostia in the building set up for Civilian Employee Assistance Program (CEAP) counseling, and where we would return there for our group counseling session later.

We piled into two cars and went off to meet the tour guide, a liaison assigned there from the Navy. He showed us around the building he worked in and through the underground tunnels that take people from one building to the next. Then he dropped us off at the tours area so we could take our tour. He met us afterward and showed us some things the tour guide didn't. We enjoyed a wonderful lunch in one of the cafeterias. While we were eating lunch, we gave our home email addresses to one of the telewokers who would be onsite more than off now, so we could get information as it came out. Then we thanked the tour guide and left for our group therapy session.

The leader of the session was asking us questions about how we felt and writing down the feelings even before we shouted them out. He explained this as our new normal; not something I was exited to hear. This told me I would be in therapy for a long time and I didn't think I'd like that. I had to leave early, but one of the therapists followed me out to let me know the crisis counseling line was always open and I could call it anytime, even months from now. That was good to know.

CHAPTER 14

Leadership Response

As I sat there at my home office desk listening in on the weekly telecom meeting, one of the rare ones I was able to attend, I was listening to our leadership provide suggestions about what we should do. The meeting started with our leadership's voicing of their main concern that people take care of themselves (counseling) and each other. I made a mental note of several points that came out, each of which focused my mind to the point of asking myself questions concerning the true care meant by leadership.

Shortly after the shooting, a representative of our group contacted one of the members who wasn't involved in the shooting. He performed most of his work via telework. He asked for our personal email addresses so he could take notes during these meetings and send them to everyone to keep the group up to date on the latest information from leadership and about the movement of people into temporary offices. The email notes of the telecom sent out to our home emails by our onsite person, although short, addressed the content of the meeting more accurately than I could, but I can decipher what I think they meant.

Points for which we were looking for answers included the following:

- If people were ready to come back to work, where would they go and who would they contact to coordinate?
- How would people get paid?
- How soon could people get their personal possessions out of Building 197?
- How soon could people get their cell phones out of the cabinet by the front doors?
- How soon could people go into their office spaces to collect work files?
- Is there a medical assistance team nearby to assist those who need it?

During this particular telecom, the suggestion came up that even if employees didn't have a computer, it was recommended they still come in just to be with the SEA-10 family. The Executive Assistant tempered that later in the conversation with her knowledge that there may not be anything for employees to do if there was no work place and no computer, so it could be frustrating. In other words, after some discussion she realized that when employees came in to work and have no computer with which to work, their minds will tend to dwell. If their minds dwell, they will settle on the shooting. This definitely would not be a good idea, but she couldn't say this to leadership, so the best she could do was temper the comment by mentioning it a little later in the meeting.

After the shooting, the Navy Yard was closed for two days while investigations continued. Our chain of command was notified that all personnel would be paid their salaries until the investigation surrounding the Building 197 shooting was completed. Of course, everyone was concerned with getting their pay, especially after having just come off furlough, so that issue had to be addressed. The announcement was made that everyone would be paid 40 hours the first week. If people could access ERP (Enterprise Resource Planning; the overall time and budget system used by Naval Sea Systems Command) they were to put in their hours, but regardless of what was entered, it appeared as though everyone was to get paid for 40 hours for the week after which adjustments *might* be necessary. Those who had vehicles on the base were told they could return to pick them up after the second day of investigation was completed. This was difficult for some who were on the fourth floor when the shooting started, but if the vehicle was their only mode of transportation, there were no other options.

For several weeks after the shooting, only one gate to the Navy Yard was open. It also happened to be the farthest gate from the Metro station. This entailed a great deal of walking, adding to the morning commute; taking more time for people to get to their offices, and creating additional stress to those handicapped people who normally make the walk from the Navy Yard Metro to the Navy Yard's first open gate; a far shorter distance. During the weekly telecoms, there was some discussion about the long lines at the single gate being used for entering and egress, and the notes our representative sent out let us know that NAVSEA was working on getting another gate open because of the long lines that were forming at that single gate each morning. After all, the rest of the Navy Yard was open for business shortly following the shooting and had to enter the one gate while all the other gates remained closed as the employees of the Yard walked by each gate.

Since personal possessions remained in Building 197, driver's licenses were being requested as proof of the items belonging to specific individuals. If DC residents didn't have their driver's licenses because their wallets were still in the building, they could request a replacement on-line. Leadership was not sure, but thought people may also be able to do that in Virginia and Maryland. Many people were interested in retreiving other personal belongings, like spare shoes, pictures, and momentos, not to mention keys to cars, wallets, purses, and bags or briefcases. The question as to whether or not people could retrieve their other belongings had not been answered by the chain of command as yet.

Since we left the building with nothing, or very little, we were concerned about getting some of our personal items back. I know there were more people in NAVSEA than just one of my employees who had to buy a throw-away phone to communicate with others. When their phones were eventually returned, they all would give up their temporary phones. The cell phones are such a necessary part of life it's hard to imagine doing anything without them, and yet they are all locked behind those glass front doors and not available to be gathered up and handed out to their owners. Hence the need for replacing them with the throw-away phones. Our leadership let it be known that we should save our receipts for items we needed to purchase in the interim between the day of the shooting and the date our items were returned to us. The receipts would be used to obtain reimbursment for our expenses later. By the tone of the meetinag, it was understood that right after the furlough period, we wouldn't have the funds to be able to purchase our own temporary equipment and leadership was making this as easy as they could for us, in spite of the lack of funds.

In one of the later telecoms, discussion surrounding the rumor that many people heard the families of the victims were allowed into the building to look at the office spaces of their loved ones to help in their healing process. The carpet tiles had been replaced and the cubicles were cleaned before this was allowed so no one saw the havoc wreaked by the shooter. Employees of the building wanted to know why the families of the victims were allowed in to see the building and the employees themselves weren't. There would be no immediate response from leadership for this query either.

The telecom did mention the availability of counselors for all of us and the location of the counselors' office. This would be mentioned in every telecom henceforth. As it turned out, there would be many people availing themselves of the counselors over the next few months. Part of the problem with our need for counseling included questions about the condition of the building after the shooting, including the possibilities of what may have led up to the shooting. Though the shooting itself didn't tear up the building, the FBI and NCIS did a great deal of damage looking for what they thought was a second shooter.

We were originally under the impression that the repairs to our building would take several months. The facility repair lead said that it would more likely take more than a year before the building would be ready for use. When the police were looking for the second shooter, they were tearing down walls and doors during the search. Amos, our facilities improvement and repair lead, said that the building will look completely different when repairs were finished, and will probably have a different entrance too. The different entrance is a good idea as most of us associate that entrance with the shooting. Psychologically, a new entrance would do wonders to eliminate that effect on those who were deeply involved with the shooting incident; especially those who headed out the front door as the chaos began.

Since the shooting started on the 4th deck and ended on the 3rd deck, there was no definite timeline on when personal items will be retrieved from the 3rd and 4th decks. These two areas were the crime scene and we knew they would be the last places to be cleared for delivery of personal items, but contrary to earlier information, we would get our personal effects before the cubicles and offices were packed for delivery to temporary office spaces, and cleared out so repairs could begin.

In an email, the Admiral recognized the hard work of crews sent in to retrieve personal items, such as wallets, purses, and items requested by personnel on forms sent in ahead of time. They were the only people allowed in the building while it was in its present condition. They were bonded and were expressly allowed to collect personal items for others so people could get their wallets, purses, and other personal effects back before the packing of the building begins. The building contents; each cubicle and office, had to be packed for movement to temporary office space so the building repairs could begin. The email follows.

The Admiral's Update on Delivery of Personal Items

[. . .] The Vice Admiral recognized the people by name who volunteered their time to make the pick up of personal effects such a success. He continued in his email to let us know the status of the personal items from Building 197:

"As for delivering items from the 2nd and 5th decks, most items have been claimed by their owners and I want to commend the superb team of people who worked over the weekend to get that work done. The material came out of the building in bags with only the cubicle number on them, and our team of facilities and security folks, supplemented by volunteers from the warfare centers and other organizations identified the owners, inventoried it and organized it to make it simple to pick up. The team of volunteers worked very hard, over 12 hours per day, over nights and through the weekend to get this job done. Over 900 bags were made up and almost 800 have been delivered. Well done to all. The hours of operations at the pick-up point in the lobby of Bldg 201, are 0700-1700 daily. We will keep you posted as we are allowed to move on to other floors."

He couldn't help but recognize the team as an entity because there were so many people from all over the Navy Yard who put in their time to make sure the personal effects of each person were handled with care. Each decision made about personal items to be packaged up for delivery to owners was made with careful consideration about where else the items could be used (other than at work). After all, some people wouldn't be coming right back to work, but might need a specific type of shoe for other functions. The same could be said for personal notebooks, and even makeup.

The Admiral went on in his email, "I would like to add my heartfelt thanks to the huge team of volunteers that made Sunday's Memorial Service so special. An interesting data point is that the typical planning time for a Presidential visit such as this is over two months, and we completed it in about 48 hours. Well done to all."

V/R
Ted
RDML Ted Kennedy

Leadership continues to let us know about the preparations for our more permanent home. The Coast Guard building at Buzzard's Point has been identified for our use over the next year. The Commanding Admiral of NAVSEA is already there and set up. He's let us know that a contractor has been hired to lay out the offices and cubicle areas. At this point it is one month later and things are moving along toward a solution for us to have new offices that are not on the Navy Yard.

Until the Coast Guard building is ready for us to occupy, some temporary offices have been set up for us on the Navy Yard, some are in Building 33, (NAVFAC), some are in building 201, Office of Civilian Human Resources (OCHR), and some are in Building 179, Commander, Naval Installation Command (CNIC). At the time, I still didn't know what building NAVFAC was in, but would work on finding that out. My next foray to the Navy Yard, I hoped, would be to get Nina into the Yard. I planned on trying the Navy Yard myself in the next week or so.

After the first week when I suffered through the night without medication, and I managed to get the phone number to the crisis line, I used it a great deal. When the FBI's Wendt Center called me with an appointment for a psychiatrist who could provide perscriptions for medications that would help me sleep and diminish the nightmares, I began to find some peace. When my children found out about the nightmares and need for medications, they got together and arranged to each spend a week at a time with me to provide someone in person to talk to when I have my nightmares. My husband is hard of hearing and couldn't hear me when I was whimpering and trying to talk at the same time. It was very difficult to talk to him without raising my voice enough to sound like I was yelling. That was enough to tire anyone out after a while.

I was already looking forward to our planned trip to visit our grandchildren in Texas, and the week was such fun I didn't want it to end. My second oldest son understands Post Traumatic Stress Disorder (PTSD), and this is the son we were visiting. He suffers from it and gave me some hints to help me through the worst bouts. However, my PTSD was still fresh so some of his hints didn't work like they should have.

The next person to come visit was my youngest son. When I needed someone to talk to, he was wonderful. He listened to my tearful nightmare stories and talked to me about anything I wanted to talk about. We stayed up nights just talking so I would calm down. My only daughter came to visit next and stayed up with me when I came to her to talk about my nightmares. It was almost like she was expecting it those nights; she hadn't yet gone to bed. It was great having her and her chihuahua visit. They're both real troopers, especially when ole' mom comes in and talks their ears off about a nightmare and then just talks to talk. Our oldest came to visit next. By this time it had been a month since the shooting and my nightmares weren't occurring multiple times each night. As a matter of fact, they weren't occurring more than a few times a week. I was getting excited about the lack of nightmares. Our oldest helped with some of the repairs around the house. He's really built and those muscles were a fantastic help lifting some of the heavy blocks and wood into place. We hated to say good-bye to each of our children when they departed.

Well, I went to the Navy Yard the day after our last child left and still suffer tremendously when going past Building 197. After that day's trip to the Navy Yard, I feel I can do it again, but may bring my husband to be the driver. Now that I can get myself to enter the Yard, I need to find out where my people are working so I can check in on them. I still have to get into that laptop, but that will come. I need to help my people get themselves straight, and then we can help each other along the path to healing.

As long as our leadership understands, we need to push forward using itty bitty baby steps so we aren't pushing too hard, but so we experience forward movement. I experienced that in the regular work-a-day world in one of my past jobs just trying to get the job done and it was my boss's favorite saying. We'll use it now and make it our motto; "itty bitty baby steps, but forward movement."

CHAPTER 15

Planning for a Future Disaster

My daughter works for a contractor at Ft. Rucker, Alabama. In light of the NAVSEA shooting, her company felt it necessary to review their disaster plan. This review was to occur in their upcoming safety assessment, which coincided with the one week anniversary of the Navy Yard shooting. She said they were going to be shown a workplace violence video and then she would be asked about complications I ran into during the Navy Yard disaster.

Since I discussed the Navy Yard and surrounding community's first response plan with my daughter, she was asked if she would mind sharing any lessons learned from my experience. She already planned on discussing the failure of their phone tree and evacuation meeting locations. She emailed me and asked if I had any other recommendations or suggestions from my experience that might help her group. I responded, but it was after 0100 a.m. and I was tired; one of my chronic problems lately.

The next morning arrived; it was a new day. Now that I had some sleep, I went back over the email with my observations and suggestions. After reading over my responses later in the morning, I decided my answers didn't all make sense. So, I made some modifications; adding and changing some items. Then I sent the corrected responses off to my daughter. The following is a recap of my reply.

First of all, I congratulated her team on pre-planning for such an occasion. I've worked in a number of locations where there was no plan and often wondered what we would be expected to do in an emergency situation. I told her the time spent conducting planning would be extremely worthwhile. One of my thoughts was that I prayed my daughter's team would never have to use the emergency plan, but if they did have to dust off that plan, even if it was only used one time, at least they would have an operational plan available. However, I recommended that they thoroughly test it out before having to implement it during a real disaster situation. Even though everything doesn't come together as planned during an actual emergency, at least shortcomings can be identified ahead of time and mitigated to the extent possible. The first issue to address would be how to know an emergency situation is occurring and the nature of the emergency.

At the Navy Yard, we didn't have so much a failure of a phone notification system. We had a ludicrous regulation that required everyone to either leave their cell phones in lock boxes at the entrances of the building or in their cars. We used to have a regulation that allowed us to buy and use non-camera phones on the job. Of course, many didn't purchase and use cameraless phones; they just hid their regular cell phones in their desk drawers so they could remain in contact with the outside world, and feel like they had close contact to their families in the case of an emergency at home. The alternative was to use the Navy phones to make necessary calls, many of which were long distance, for which the Navy was charged. When the new regulation came out, it forced our staff to make personal calls on the Navy's dime. As you can imagine, most of us had a problem with this new regulation!

When I was looking to muster my employees, boss, and co-workers, I couldn't find them because their cell phones were in the lock boxes! Worse, some had phones in their cars, which they couldn't get to because the garage was cordoned off and no access was allowed for at least 24 hours. The people who were allowed access to their cars the next day were able to retrieve their cell phones. However, those phones locked in the lockboxes, just feet away from the entrance doors, were unretrievable for weeks. Many people had to buy GoPhones, the cheap throw-away phones, just to be able to communicate with family in an emergency because they didn't own house phones. I'm sure this was not something the police thought of, nor did the people who developed the regulation. What this regulation did was to put people at risk by sending them on to rally points, and eventually home, without any means of communication.

I would say the phone notification system would work for those individuals outside the immediate area, and in the absence of a regulation that required the confiscation of cell phones at the building entrances. But, when running for your life, would you really remember to grab your cell phone? Unless you're wearing your phone, chances are you'd leave it and run for your life. My employee was shot at from four feet away. When the shooter was forced to reload his weapon, she ran away and had no time to grab her purse, or anything else. She just left. I would too. Fixing the phone notification system would be nice, but there needs to be a backup plan too. A plan A and a plan B. Come up with that and you would most likely have an optimal solution. During the 911 phone call, consider what to say to the operator. You should identify the type of emergency: shooting, bomb threat, explosion, poison gas, tornado, etc. This would help convey the critical information needed by first responders as quickly as possible so the operator can get the right assistance to you as rapidly as possible.

Another confusing issue that cropped up was which 911 dispatcher was supposed to be connected to the Navy Yard telephone system. Supposedly, when we call 911 from the phones on our desks, we're understood to be connected with the Navy Yard police. When we call from our cell phones, the call is supposed to connect with the DC police department. When I called 911, I gave my name, building number, and floor where the shooter was located. Since I was calling from my desk phone, I wasn't worried about reporting where in Washington D.C. the problem was occurring because I was calling, or so I thought, the Navy Yard 911 operator. Wrong!

The operator asked where Building 197 was. I was shocked. I expected to be talking to the Navy Yard 911 police dispatcher. Wrong again! I had to tell her it was on the Navy Yard! We were mis-informed from day one about which agency was handling our emergency 911 calls! So, I recommended that she be sure about where 911 calls are connected. If the 911 operation is outside the military base, then the caller has to let the 911 operator know that the emergency is on the base and explain any specifics about the location and situation so the operator can react properly. If there is only one central 911 operations center, it would be very helpful for them to be trained on and to have detailed floor plans on file for ready reference. These plans should have all buildings numbered so the operator can identify which building is involved in the emergency. Detailed floor plans may not be needed for years, but when they are needed, they would be invaluable to first responders. When I say detailed, I mean detailed, to the seat, cubicle, and office number. Of course classified building information would be the exception. This would allow the operator to relay specific information to law enforcement personnel, firefighters, and ambulance response teams.

As a result, when a person talking to 911 states, "He's on the other side of my cubicle," the operator will already know where the caller is located and can easily point the police liaison (whom in my case was standing next to her) to the location of the shooter. He can then relay the information to his police and SWAT teams who then can more easily determine a shooter's location. After all, not every shooter will stay in one place for a matter of minutes like the Navy Yard shooter did, but they all stand in one place thinking of their next move for a short duration of time. This shooter just happened to stay on the other side of my cubicle for more than 'a few' minutes.

It isn't clear who set off the fire alarm in the building, but what is clear is that it should never have been activated because it added considerably to the overall confusion. Fire alarms are for fires and should be reserved for that purpose. Other methods should be used to communicate different emergency situations. For instance, in addition to fire alarms, we have distinctive sirens that provide tornado warnings, security alarms that provide unique alerts, characteristic civil defense air raid sirens, and the ubiquitous Civil Defense Message warble. It seems we could decide on an emergency situation warning to cover internal security breaches such as during a shooting type incident. Coupled with the warning should be a decidedly detailed set of broadcasted messages to guide individuals during the emergency. Additionally, messages should not be contradictory like they were during the Navy Yard shooting incident; fist telling people to exit the building, then telling them to shelter in place.

Another consideration is to have a detailed rally point outside the building in an evacuation situation such as a fire. However, there should be attention given to what to do and where to run in the case of a violent-incident evacuation. Certainly, the normal outside-the-building muster may not be suitable. This plan will take some thought and perhaps some coordination with local first response teams. It may not be needed for years, but when it is needed, it will be invaluable.

When the police entered Building 197 at the Navy Yard, they had no clue as to the layout of the facility. Their situational awareness was further hindered because the Navy Yard guards would not leave their posts to accompany them through the building. They are required to stay at their posts, but by doing that, they impeded the search for the shooter. A solution would have been to activate all the guards (those on break, nearby, or leave a skeleton crew the gate and elsewhere, etc.) to provide assistance to the police. This could have been done within 3 minutes; certainly by the time the police arrived.

The flooring for offices and decks around the atrium were put into place around the cranes, hooks, and girders that were a part of the original factory building. There were places where the floors were laid that had girders coming right down to the side of the balcony and there were file cabinets butted right up against the girders; both the angled and straight girders. As a consequence, the police lost the shooter several times because they didn't realize there were so many hiding places in the building. At one time, Building 197 was used to make the 16-inch guns, and the cranes and girders used to support those operations are still in place. Cranes built to hold that size of gun through the forging process are huge and the girders that hold those cranes in place are angled to the "floor" and below to provide maximum weight capacity for those cranes. This layout provides a perfect hiding place for someone who wishes to keep out of sight.

In Building 197 there are nooks and crannies in unexpected places where someone who knew the layout of the building could hide. Civilian police who would not have access to buildings on the Navy Yard would not be familiar with the layout of any of the buildings, much less this one. The Navy Yard guards would have been able to point out potential hiding places to the police during their search for the shooter, and may have helped part of the time, but not from the moment the police initially entered the building. After all, I was providing information to the 911 operator and heard her as she began to relay the information to the officer standing near her. With that information, it would have been easy for guards to show the police where I was hearing the shots and to direct them to the appropriate locations. Instead of being constrained by some unthought-out regulations that imobilized the guards in Building 197, plans should be created and thoroughly tested that allow them to be more flexible and helpful.

Another issue was how law enforcement applied their rules of engagement in the shooting situation. When the police yelled, "Stop! Police! Put your hands up!" Did they really think someone who just killed several people would actually stop and surrender? At the Navy Yard, the shooter's response was to fire at them. They returned fire, but as soon as he shot at them, and before they got off their first shot, he'd turned around and began running. As a result, he would get away. The sounds of him running down the hallway could be heard throughout the building. The police couldn't run fast enough, or couldn't see where he turned to escape their tail, and he got away; numerous times. After several minutes more, the police found him, and again yelled at him to "Stop! ..." with the same response each time. Even though they shot back at him, he ran away and they lost him. This senerio played out several times! Their response to finding him was the same each time, "Stop! Police! Put your hands up!" At some point, law enforcement should have made the decision to shoot first and asked questions later! My opinion is that the change in modus operandi should have been right after the first instance of having return fire in response to the "Stop! Police! Put your hands up!" order. Maybe the guard killed by the shooter would still be alive if the police fired first instead of issuing a verbal warning. I also think the shooter wouldn't have been able to wrest the gun away from a guard either. As it turned out, the shooter was able to arm himself with both his shotgun and a pistol. A discussion about the police response to a shooting situation is suggested; with the

Military Police, and perhaps the civilian police departments supporting your Army post might yield a faster transition from the verbal response phase to a more aggressive response on the second encounter with a shooter and might minimize the number of fatalities.

One expected issue that became apparent and needs to be sorted out, is how the shooter was able to obtain and maintain a secret clearance with his background. Failure of the background check and reporting process somewhere along the security clearance chain indicated a catastrophic system failure. As a result, not all of the shooter's short- and long-term security breaches were reported to proper authorities. He should never have passed the background check. This isn't something that can be handled at the local level. However, it is something local agencies need to be concerned about. What local people can do though is to report anomalous behavior inconsistent with what would normally be expected of individuals holding security clearances. It is especially important for businesses that have employees with security clearances to better monitor their behavior. All this requires training and awareness similar to corporate safety programs.[11]

Consider the layout of the building when answering the following questions as the layout may have an impact on the way you develop your answers. Think about what your immediate reaction to the various emergency events would or should be. Consider what the reaction of others should or would be. What should the reaction be? Determine the reaction and then practice it.

---

[11] Defense officials acknowledged that a lot of red flags were missed in Alexis' background, allowing him to maintain a secret-level security clearance and access to our Navy installation despite a string of behavioral problems and brushes with the law prior to his arrival at the Navy Yard. He was even counseled just the week prior in his new position. But without knowledge of the red flags, how was his new employer to know it wasn't just a problem adjusting to his new work environment? For the Safety workshop, there isn't much that can be done with this information.

The shooter worked for The Experts, a Florida-based computer firm that was a subcontractor to Hewlett-Packard. The fact that Hewlett-Packard is severing ties with The Experts, results from their supposed failing to respond adequately to Alexis' mental problems and other reported security shortfalls. These shorcomings only came to light after the shooting. How is it the supervisor didn't know of this incident? What went wrong in this case that allowed this incident to occur without notification to the customer, NAVSEA? The Experts had a responsibility and they failed in that responsibility. This failure was identified by authorities as one aspect of what ultimately cost 12 people their lives. Your team may not have direct control over contractor background security clearances, but your team does have a responsibility for reporting behavior inconsistent with security policies. Be cognizant of unusual behavior, especially in new contractors and employees; there may be more under the surface.

There is no accounting for the possibility that someone may fail to report a felony just as was the case with the Navy Yard shooter. Your planning has to encompass those things your team can influence and act upon. Anybody, regardless of security checks, can go postal at any time. Your job is to plan for what happens when this occurs. What do you do during a potential shooting event? Afterward? How should you communicate with peers? What about the 911 operator? How about the law enforcement officials, etc.? Put these plans in place and then practice them to ensure employees know what's expected of them. Then make changes when and where appropriate.

Another point is how the shooter managed to smuggle a shotgun into the building. The security video taken on the day of the shooting shows him casually slinging a bag over his shoulder. It was slung in such a manner so as to not provide a hint to the guard there may be something under his arm and down his side. His casual demeanor failed to raise suspicion in the guards when he walked in the building.

The guards had no idea that he may be carrying a deadly weapon. The sensors didn't go off because he most likely had the weapon high enough so it couldn't be detected by the not-quite-waist-high-sensors, which proved to be another failure in the system.

The evacuation was quick for those individuals who could get out when the shooting started. It was fortunate the buildings across the base provided shelter for us with no questions asked. That wasn't a problem. The base was locked down so no one could leave by vehicle or on foot. This was more of a problem for the people on the base who weren't working in Building 197. Once the shooter was neutralized and the immediate threat subsided, the base was still not opened for egress. This is something to think about. Does the base need to stay closed or not? Our problem was the possibility of a second shooter and the need to ensure the status of that possibility.

The Navy Captain in charge of the building where I ended up was very accommodating and opened his building to us. The shooting started at 0815 a.m. and people were still evacuating until noon. From shortly after the shooting started, there were at least 3,000 people who had no access to a cafeteria or the coffee shops for lunch. Captain Theodore's employees scavenged through their desk drawers to find foodstuffs. They had to know we'd be hungry after hours with nothing to eat or drink. Since the base was closed no one could make food runs and we were in our sanctuary until 7:00 p.m. Think of an emergency supply of food and water and include that in the emergency plan. The plan should account for the largest group or building on the base that may be affected. How will you feed them because they may be there for an undetermined amount of time? In our case it was up to 10 hours. If food and water are going to be part of an evacuation plan, consider the need to recycle the rations at or before their expriation date. There should be enough emergency water on hand to feed the occupants of the largest building for 24 hours. On military bases, Meals Ready to Eat (MRE) may be the way to go.

Another issue was lack of telephones for people to contact their families. Since we had no cell phones available to contact loved ones, it was apparent that telephones be made available to affected people. In our sanctuary building the Captain recognized this and had phones set up where there were active lines installed. He opened offices where there were no employees. Many of his employees opened their offices and phone lines to anyone who wanted to use them. There were even phone chargers brought out for Smartphones. Unfortunately, I didn't have a Smartphone, so my dead battery remained uncharged. There were enough phone lines in this building, but there were other buildings with far fewer lines. I used a land line to call out and had people calling in to me while I was trying to locate my employees.

The Captain also recognized that we were in his building with no news from the outside. He had a computer set up through the intenet to receive the television news. The system was connected to the large screens in the conference room so we could see the latest news. He even had the latest news broadcast over the speakers for those who weren't in the conference room. Keeping the people informed was paramount and should be considered in your plan. This helps keep your people situationally aware of what is happening while awaiting further instructions. I didn't realize it until that day, but not knowing is worse than knowing, even if we are being fed incorrect information.

Another consideration is a central muster list at a designated central operation center on the base. Every building that harbors evacuees needs to have a muster list of people it has taken in, but more importantly, there needs to be a centrally designated place that gathers the lists, or a copy, and puts them into a master list. That way when someone is looking for a missing person, the designated central list can be referred to by all who need to muster their personnel. Some of the people who saw the shooter or encountered him were rescued by NCIS or the FBI and were debriefed by them immediately. They were taken home by the FBI after the base opened for buses to go to the stadium with their load of people who'd finished interviews by the FBI. This was an action taken by the FBI in deference to the ordeal those people had been through, and because their cars were in lockdown in the garage across from Building 197. So rather than have these people go through even more of an ordeal trying to get home while their cars are left on the base, the FBI took them home so they could begin some form of a normal evening in familiar surroundings. However, the rest of the people from Building 197 who needed to make their way home were provided with a different transportation plan.

Finally, transportation of masses of people out of harm's way needs to be considered. We had to give our statements to the FBI. Granted it takes a while for 3,000 people to give their statements, but most of the people in Building 197 didn't see or hear anything. At first, FBI interviews of the 3,000 plus people were detailed. Toward the end of the process, the FBI started asking just one question, whether you saw or heard anything. If the answer was no, you were sent on your way. The FBI could have asked individuals where they were located during the shooting. Floor by floor the FBI could have eliminated an estimated 2,000 people right away. Then they could have eliminated another 500 by asking on what side of Building 197 they worked or where they were at 0815 a.m. that morning. Continuing on, once particular information was obtained by the FBI, individuals were sent outside to load onto buses. A little communication between FBI and police would be very helpful in reducing the wait time between evacuation of a building and evacuation of the base. The buses sat in the line waiting to get full before heading off. Directions could have been to fill the first bus in line then head to the second bus in line so the first bus could move out, but those directions were never given. As a result, we had four buses only partially filled and all were waiting to get full before moving. In some cases the buses at the end of the line were full and couldn't move because the first three buses weren't full yet. A little logistics here would have made for a smoother exit strategy, and smaller bottleneck of people waiting for the next group of buses to pull up.

One advantage of being associated with the Navy Yard is the ability to contract for buses with little advanced notice. The drivers of many buses were Marines. They were sent from Quantico to assist. On the Army post the capability to contract for after-hours bus transportation may be just as quickly done as it was with the Navy, and may even be accomplished with a task order as it was between the Navy and Marines. However, without advanced planning, one won't know for sure, so advance preparation ensures the proper paperwork is completed in time to use the buses if the time should occur that they are needed. The reason for us to be taken off of the base was for us to be able to be met by family and friends for rides home at the stadium. Those of us who could not be met were directed to wait for a bus to receive a task order to take people to commuter parking lots south of the city along I-95 where their cars were located. Many people lived in nearby commuting areas where neighbors and friends or family members could come to pick them up. So the size of the crowd expanded and contracted as buses departed and returned with new loads of survivors and family members came to pick up their loved-ones from the crowd to take them home.

Planning in advance where to bus people off base where they can recoup themselves and plan for getting home was done at the last minute. Luckily it worked out pretty smoothly. The Nationals canceled their game on this day because of the shooting at the Navy Yard. They also offered a side of their stadium as a mustering point for the buses to drop people off to wait for further directions about getting to their commuter lots and homes. This gave authorities access to a large area for a great many people that could be easily cordoned off and guarded. Once the planning began, it only took a matter of hours to affect a solution. The Red Cross was called and they did what they do best: provide comfort, distribute blankets, and feed the hungry. One never thinks of this kind of thing happening in your own back yard, but once the shooter was neutrtalizied, the police from the Tri-state area answered the call to assist, buses were commandeered from the Marine base, and charter buses were contracted to transport us to the stadium. The only nearby facility big enough to handle the number of evacuees was the Nationals stadium. It's a good thing this didn't happen during the winter because we were standing outside in the entrance area of the north side of the stadium. But it was big enough to fit all of us, seven bus loads at a time.

The outpouring of love and help I received was phenomenal. After initially not being able to find help, I was finally able to get counseling and was put in touch with a psychiatrist who could provide the help I needed. The first order of business was to get me through the night without waking up every hour from my nightmares. The next order of business was to get rid of the nightmares, either the night time or daytime ones. Then we would work on the other ones. With any luck, I'd be able to get rid of the nightmares eventually. If Ft. Rucker people ran into a violent situation, the nightmares some may experience will need to be treated. Having a plan in place for stress treatment, and possibly PTSD follow-on treatment should be addressed in the plan. After-action counseling is an important consideration.

CHAPTER 16

Additional Thoughts

Changes do need to be made on several fronts to prepare for an emergency in the future. They need to be made in the reporting system. Background checks need to be more thoroughly investigated to keep unqualified people from slipping through the cracks and getting a clean bill of mental health. One way to make sure the right information gets to the Defense Security Service for the examiner to review is to ensure the information is correct when it is placed on the forms. When auditors track the completeness of the information it would be helpful if the law enforcement agencies that were involved in cases with the application interviews made more accurate statements concerning the applicant. To ensure this, law enforcement officers who are less than honest in their reporting on these forms need to be held accountable. Total accountability and responsibility would ensure enforcement officer investigators review all records to ensure applicants are providing honest responses to the questions on the forms. Gross oversights and errors in judgment should be career-enders for an investigator. If you think that is too harsh, think back to the Navy Yard shootings and count the number of careers that were ended because of a law enforcement officer's failure to report a felony; a security clearance breaking felony, that would have kept the Navy Yard shooter out of Building 197 and off of the Navy Yard. Clearer responses to questions about previous employees would allow decisions to be made at the appropriate level about whether to allow a secret clearance or not. This alone would go a long way to "fix" the workplace violence problem.

Barring the background check success, make sure everyone knows where the 911 call goes. If it goes off base, we should know that. That means there is only one 911 center. If so, then it isn't out of the ordinary for the Center to have blueprints of all the government buildings, and larger non-government buildings in the Tri-State area under lock and key. In the unusual event they are needed, they can be pulled out for reference, expediting the location of any perpetrator.

If the building is large and the police come in, make sure they come in with the guards that are familiar with that building and the intricacies of the building layout. In the case of Building 197, there were enough places where the shooter could hide that the Navy Yard guards would have been helpful if consulted sooner.

When the police see the shooter, I presume they are required to yell a warning. As such, the first time they see a perpetrator, they yell "Stop! Police! Put your hands up!" This is understood as protocol. However, after realizing that the shooter shoots back instead of putting his hands up on the first encounter, there should not be two more encounters with the same verbal instruction. The next encounter should have been to shoot first and ask questions later. Doing this would, of course, deny the police the opportunity to question the shooter, but would have saved countless lives by stopping him dead in his tracks. In my book saving additional lives beats trying to capture the shooter alive for questioning.

In planning for a disaster, we should consider the situations and the root causes to prepare for any disaster and make it easier to follow a disaster plan, when and if it's ever needed, again. I'll list the most salient of situations and work toward the Root Cause to demonstrate possible solutions. There are other, less critical issues that could be added to my list, but to fix the problem or address a developing plan, this will be a good beginning.

The "sensors" need to go all the way up to the full height of a person and they need to be metal detectors. Similar systems in other government buildings perform full-body scans for metal, so why not in our building? That alone would have caught the metal of the shotgun, either in pieces in the bag slung casually over the shoulder, or hung under the arm of the shooter and hidden by the bag used as a distractor.

During the evacuation, a representative in each building took the names of survivors and placed them on muster lists, but there was no master muster list generated. If there was, I wouldn't have been looking for my employee for two hours and wouldn't have had to have her declared missing. There needs to be a responsibility assigned to one building for keeping a master muster list and all other buildings need to know who has this responsibility so they can report their muster lists to that building's representative. Logic dictates the largest building have this responsibility simply because the other buildings would, without a doubt already know which is the largest building, and therefore, which building would have that responsibility.

There was no need for the FBI to interview all 3,000 people who worked in Building 197. Eliminating those who worked or were sequestered on the seaside wing immediately would have saved immense time. Knowing the fourth, third, and first floors were involved would logically allow for those who worked on those floors to be asked if they evacuated the building when the alarm went off, and and then make interview decisions from those responses. Obviously, the majority who immediately evacuated didn't see anything, but may have heard the first one or two shots. Those who were evacuated later may need to be questioned, but the list of employees who needed to be questioned would now be closer to around 1,500 rather than 3,000.

Since the police and FBI were looking for a second shooter after the first shooter was neutralized, another look at the situation might be warranted. The employees who left the building closer to noon should definitely be questioned, even if they insist they didn't see or hear anything. In this case, they may be the very people who should be questioned. After all, we were told by the media and Captain Theodore that the FBI and NCIS were looking for a second shooter. When faced with the possibility of a second shooter, nothing should be taken for granted. It should be noted that an excellent way for a second person to escape is for him or her to act as if s/he were a part of the same group that was accosted by the original shooter, thus effecting her/his escape. By questioning those who came out last, the FBI has a chance to catch any perpetrators who might try that method of escape. Matching those who have ID cards to their faces also helps keep the system honest by ensuring people's faces actually do match the face on the ID.

Transportation off base was well planned. The use of buses was orderly and efficient considering it was the first time they were used in an actual emergency situation, and there were a few glitches here and there. However, planning for transportation to the commuter lots for those of us stranded at the National's Stadium was not planned in advance and I have to wonder how it would have gone if I stayed to wait for that elusive bus. I was very lucky that Ubercars volunteered rides home for those with cars in commuter lots. It was a long day and I was definitely ready to head home. Using the Situation, Task, Action, Results, Root Cause and Recommendation (STARR) model we can identify the problems in each situation and dig down to the root cause of each problem. Once we've identified the root cause, almost always not a person, but rather a systemic problem, we can recommend the changes to make to mitigate those problems in the future.

Calling the 911 Operator:

SITUATION: The emergency- what to say to the operator and who should call.

TASK: Some emergencies are obvious, like a fire, or flood. But sometimes, emergencies aren't easily identified by an entire building. In some cases, like a bomb threat, usually called in to one person, or a shooting, usually heard by several dozen people, someone needs to call 911. Who should that be?

ACTIONS: Since 911should be called immediately and there isn't time to hold a conference to determine who should call, either a pre-appointed person should be assigned well in advance of any emergency, or, barring that, persons with the capability should call 911. When I called 911, it didn't dawn on me to ask if there were others who'd called in, but when I finally did ask, the operator told me I was the only person still on the line with them.

RESULTS: The operator will tell you when there are others who are providing information. You will either be providng information to 911 that is required, or 911 will let you know there are others providing information already.

ROOT CAUSE ANALYSIS: The root cause of the problem was the fact that I was providing information to the operator from a single position so there was no method of triangulating the data to allow the police to make more accurate choices on possible locations of the shooter. Having more data points would have provided a better overall picture to police for them to make their decisions on movments to capture or neutralize the shooter.

RECOMMENDATIONS: Not only allow cell phones, but have them be attached to our belts when we are away from our desks to avoid the lack of cell phones upon sudden evacuation so the 911 operator could be getting more information than from the few people left in the building. This would serve two purposes; allow information to flow into the 911 dispatchers from multiple sources allowing for better decision making on the part of the first responders, and make mustering easier for those of us who are concerned about our friends and co-workers who were directly involved with the shooter and were no longer in the area.

Evacuation procedures:

SITUATION: The evacuation procedures for wounded and non-wounded and ensuring evacuation is complete.

TASK: Personnel, who are able, need to be evacuated in some emergency situations. Determining which situations require evacuation and which require secure in place.

ACTIONS: Determine what the procedures are for evacuating wounded and non-wounded personnel during an emergency.

RESULTS: Once the plan is in place for evacuating personnel during an emergency, it should be practiced. If the base is closed, other buildings on the base will be required to take in the evacuees.

ROOT CAUSE ANALYSIS: Buildings were not prepared to take in the numbers of people they did or to feed them. There was no way to know how long the people would be in these evacuation buildings and no plan in place for their care. In spite of this situation, the tenants of the building managed to come up with enough junk food, soda, fruits, and water to keep hunger at bay for 10 hours. Smaller buildings may not have fared so well and plans should take this into consideration.

RECOMMENDATIONS: Set up emergency canned food stash against an emergency evacuation situation. Water can be held in a gallon container from the sink and dispensed into disposable cups. Option: allow "food runs" from each building to pick up food from a store/fast food restaurant to feed the evacuees. This would require runs off of and back onto the base, but should be considered.

Rally points:

SITUATION: After leaving Building 197, there were police along the roads pointing us further along the roads to different points and to different buildings. There was a muster list at the front desk in the sanctuary building establishing accountability, as there surely must have been in each building that took in evacuees. The release from these buildings would not occur without the FBI's OK.

TASK: There may not be police to point personnel to other buildings during evacuation, but there will be a need for evacuation.

ACTIONS: Determine who will be in charge of guiding the evacuees to their evacuee buildings. The logical agency to guide the civilian population to their sanctuary buildings is the City or County Police or Military Police.

RESULTS: By coordinating with the police for organizing and guiding the civilian population to their evacuation buildings, the police will already be able to complete their tasks without having to learn them and they are easily identifiable to the civilian population by their uniforms.

ROOT CAUSE ANALYSIS: Using police to guide the evacuees to the buildings that were accepting people gave the evacuees a sense of security. It also ensured cooperation; after all, the police were carrying weapons. When we arrived at our sanctuary buildings, the commander of the building was the person who we listened to as he was providing us with updates, and letting us know when it was time to walk down the road to the Conference Center for our FBI interview. He was also walking around to make sure all were taken care of and he was seen by all. He was in easy reach of anyone who needed his help.

RECOMMENDATIONS: Continue using police to guide evacuees to their sanctuary buildings. FBI will continue to manage the emergency situation and questioning of evacuees prior to their leaving the base. Each building continues to be managed by the building commander, and each commander continues to keep their guests apprised of the situation occurring outside. By doing this, the evacuees are informed and less anxious about their situation; therefore willing to listen when asked to do something by the Captain or FBI.

Accountability:

SITUATION: Lack of formal accountability procedures and available call rosters. For example, when we got to our rally sanctuary, there was no procedure for obtaining the status of our employees, peers, etc. No one had personal cell phones because they were locked in cars or lockboxes, and so I couldn't go through call rosters. There was no master muster list.

TASK: Each rally point should have had a formal roster that evacuees had to sign upon arrival or reporting in, and there should have been a centralized muster list that could have been consulted for lost personnel.

ACTIONS: Accountability was hit or miss at best and there was no assured cross coordination with other rally points to consolidate lists.

RESULTS: Supervisors had no situational awareness over their subordinates, nor any visibility over peers or other missing office workers. Also, law enforcement officials had no accountability of who was and was not still in the building. At one point 911 had to be recalled to inform them of the location of a group holed up in a training room, long after the neutralization of the shooter.

ROOT CAUSE ANALYSIS: The root cause of the problem was the lack of a systematic process for accountability because there was no formal process in place for muster rosters, which couldn't be coordinated because of the unavailability of a central reporting center. I spent 2 hours looking for my supervisor, a peer, and one of my employees. I had to call 911 to have the police rescue my supervisor and co-worker from the training room. My employee was still missing, but one of our teleworkers assisted in finding her. The teleworker found out my employee was safe through a call to her mother, who lived in another state. The first call my missing employee made was to her mother, to let her her know she was safe. So as our teleworking employee began finding and calling people in the hometown of my employee, she found her mother and so found my employee was alive and well.

RECOMMENDATIONS: Make your recommendation based on the outcome of the Root Cause Analysis (RCA) and that will employ specific solutions to the problem and mitigate the issue in the future.

Transportation:

SITUATION: Transportation needed to be considered from our sanctuary to the Conference Center and then from the Conference Center to the National's Stadium. From there we were unsure about how to get to our homes, commuter lots, or what other modes of transportation were available for us to utilize where we could continue on our way home.

TASK: To the Conference Center we walked; the base is small enough to walk if you're not wearing heels. Since the base was closed and no people or vehicles were allowed in or out, the only way to get out was to take one of the buses scheduled for this purpose.

ACTIONS: The buses that took people out of the Navy Yard only left from the Conference Center. The drivers observed where we came from. If we didn't line up from the Conference Center they would reject us.

RESULTS: The buses were contracted from Quantico and by civilian companies. These were done within one day so by the end of the day we were transported to the National's Stadium.

ROOT CAUSE ANALYSIS: The buses were easy enough for the Navy to procure because the contract was in place for buses and Quantico was so near. However, there could have been a larger number of buses. With more buses there could have been some buses enlisted to take people to the different commuter lots in two groups, dropping off at each commuter lot on the way out until the bus was empty and could return for a second, and most likely, last trip south.

RECOMMENDATIONS: The system for contracting buses should be re-examined, and task orders need to be produced for making runs to the commuter lots and other modes of transportation after the first several relays of people were delivered to the stadium, thus allowing the area to thin of waiting people faster and help them get on their way home faster.

Care of evacuees:

SITUATION: 3,000 people were taken in by several buildings across the Navy Yard. What preparations were made for them for sustenance?

TASK: Evacuees were in their sanctuaries for 10 or more hours, and no one was allowed on or off the base, but there was no way to feed the 3,000 people who were evacuated. While water was fairly easy to find, there were no other buildings than Building 197 that contained a cafeteria to feed the number of people we had in our sanctuary buildng, and the food machines in our building ran out quickly.

ACTIONS: The people working in the building I sheltered in provided their stash of food and drinks to help fend off hunger. When we got to the stadium the Red Cross took over.

RESULTS: Though we had some food while we were in our sanctuary, after 10 hours, we were hungry again. The Red Cross was at the stadium with blankets to keep us warm as night settled in, and food and water to satisfy our hunger.

ROOT CAUSE ANALYSIS: In an emergency situation, no one thinks of supplying food, or how many people might be taking shelter in various buildings. There is no way to tell how long people will be in the sanctuary buildings. The systemic failure of considering the "care and feeding" of evacuees was done very well by the Red Cross and it's their forte. Allowing the Red Cross into the base/post to serve food to the evacuees should have been a consideration.

RECOMMENDATIONS: If no one is allowed off the base then the Red Cross should be able to come on the base to complete their mission. If that can't be considered, then food runs by appointed personnel, or even the Red Cross, should be in the emergency plan. Some people are diabetic and require food at certain times of the day, at the very least, medical considerations should be considered for feeding masses of people being held for half a day without being allowed to leave the base for food. One more consideration might be to allow food trucks to come onto the base and park outside each building for several minutes until they've allowed each member of the populace to purchase something to eat. Consideration must be given to those who left the building without funds, so purchasing food for the populace in this situation must also be considered; after all, this is an emergency situation.

Communications:

SITUATION: Evacuees feel confined when they're placed in a building from which they can't leave. They want to know what is happening on the outside of the building and around the base.

TASK: Evacuees need to be informed of current events to keep them up to date on the information as it is coming out to the public, and let them know they aren't sequestered with no news from the "outside."

ACTIONS: The Captain of our building kept us informed of the situations that were occurring as he was finding out or as they were occurring. We would then hear them from the media he had brought through to the conference room's large screens. He wanted us to know everything there was to know as soon as he knew it. Any employee who came in with additional information, or when the FBI provided information to him, he turned right around and announced it to us.

RESULTS: Because we were included in all information as it came out in the news or as the Captain was made aware of it, we didn't feel like we were ostrasized from the rest of the base.

ROOT CAUSE ANALYSIS: The system didn't necessarily consider informing the evacuees about what was happening. The independent thinking of the person in charge of the building we were in, instinctively knew that we would want to know what was happening with the shooter, our building, our cars, what the plans were for us to get off the base, and not only for our immediate futures, but also the following day. The system didn't consider this information necessary enough to have a plan for communicating this to each of the buildings. If the system had this consideration in place, I, as a supervisor, would have been aware of it. This information was being brought around by the FBI or NCIS agents as plans were being developed.

RECOMMENDATIONS: A system needs to be in place that considers the human nature of the need to know. During evacuations, the news needs to be made available to those evacuated, and announcements of updates need to be made as well, and they need to be made as soon as the building commander is aware of them.

Counseling:

SITUATION: Counseling was needed immediately after the incident and at various times after the incident, from a day to a week or more afterward. Not everyone was informed of the availability of counseling.

TASK: Those who needed counseling weren't immediately notified of the availability of counseling services.

ACTIONS: Some of the evacuees who experienced contact with the shooter in one way or another, and needed counseling immediately, were not contacted by the FBI's Wendt Center counselors to let them know of the availability of their counseling services.

RESULTS: Some evacuees suffered for up to a week or more until they contacted others who were being counseled by the Wendt Center counselors and received the critical phone numbers of the 24/7 emergency counseling services.

ROOT CAUSE ANALYSIS: The system did not allow for everyone who needed it to receive the phone numbers for the 24 hour crisis center causing some people to suffer needlessly without someone to talk to about their nightmares and sleeplessness. The system failed.

RECOMMENDATIONS: Provide everyone who goes through an emergency situation the number for the crisis center so they are aware of the availability of help, and ensure the information is included in the emergency plan.

All Clear:

SITUATION: Who gives all clear notification? What is the all clear notification?

TASK: The all clear notification needs to be given once the building is clear or emergency is over. The all clear notification should be easily identifiable by the evacuees.

ACTIONS: FBI partnered with NCIS but it was the FBI that had command of our situation, and only the FBI was authorized to give the all clear notification. In our case, FBI provided notification to the building commanders to move down the street to the Conference Center, and gave directions about what was to be done once we arrived there. There was no all clear given for us to leave. All personnel were to leave by bus from the Conference Center, and coordination was being performed with each building's commander by the FBI.

RESULTS: Command was clear. FBI were the only ones taking interviews, but NCIS assisted in monitoring those who were walking to the Conference Center.

ROOT CAUSE ANALYSIS: By observation, it was clear the FBI was in charge, but there was no order or message that placed them in charge. Since there was nothing in writing that placed the FBI in command, some people were absolutely sure NCIS was in charge.

RECOMMENDATIONS: Provide the name of the agency to be in charge during specific emergencies. All personnel should be aware of the information before any emergency situations occur. A plan needs to consider what agency will be in charge of the base and why; and provide a listing of other agencies that can proavide assistance in specific emergencies.

Following the STARR system we can identify numerous systemic problems that contributed to the event. Among those are lack of identification for responsibilities, procedures to be taken and when they should have been taken, evacuation process, accountability of specific agencies particular to the geographical area, communication needs of the evacuees, needs of the evacuees, transportation required for whom and when, who has responsibilty for sounding the all clear and what the all clear sounds like (and advanced knowledge to all base personnel of who that person or group is), and after-emergency situation counseling as well as location of counselors. By identifying at least these systemic responsibilities, the surprises and last minute planning can be eliminated and those needs and risks that arise during specific emergencies can have more attention paid to them.

CHAPTER 17

Epilogue

It has been four weeks since the shooting. My husband took me onto the Navy Yard yesterday because it was a holiday and traffic would be minimal. He knew if I had trouble returning to the site of the shooting, there would be few people around to witness my reaction. Since I had not been back to the Navy Yard except to drive by it, we first drove by the Yard on M Street. We had to drive by three times. Then, rather than drive by again and raise suspicion by the front entrance security guards, he made a left turn between the Navy Yard and the Department of Transportation Building. He drove me down this road for a little bit and turned into a construction area where a new building was being constructed in what used to be a part of the Navy Yard. Surprisingly, there was no fence in place and no barricade across the road.

Next, with no fence or barrier in place, we continued to drive down the side street right up to the corner of Building 197. This was cathartic for me and I cried uncontrollably. I pointed to the door where I exited and started to go down the steps toward the water when a policeman called out to me to come back toward him on the corner. My husband pulled into a parking spot right across the alley from the building. We sat there and I looked at the building. I looked at the loading dock doors where the contractors had their trucks parked when the alarm went off. I looked at the wall where I ran and walked along, from one police officer to the next until I reached the street that ran in front of Building 197, Isaac Hull Avenue, before finally crossing it.

I looked up at the fourth floor of my former office building and pointed to it. Even though I worked in the middle of the building, the fourth floor was the fourth floor and we were used to walking all over that floor on occassion. When our restrooms were being cleaned by the custodial staff, we came down to this side of the building to use the restrooms. We were familiar with this section of the fourth floor just as well as we were with our section on the other side of the building.

Then my husband pulled out of the parking spot and moved farther away into a spot that allowed me to take in the full view of the entire side of the building through the windshield. He parked straight-on so I could view the building through the windshield instead of through my passenger window. The building looked big. It was big. This was a huge building in which the shooter chose to attack people. I suppose the enormous size provided the shooter with some anonymity. Certainly, he knew many of the government and contractor personnel working in the building and the building itself undoubtedly provided many places in which to take cover.

After a few minutes of sitting in the parking lot, my husband pulled away and drove around to the front of the Navy Yard before finally turning into the entrance. This was hard for me and I think the guard could tell. We slowly drove by the front of Building 197. There were guards at the far end of the building along the waterfront. We stopped there to ask them some questions. There were tears rolling down my face by this time. I opened the window and told the guards that I used to work in that building before the shooting and that this was my first trip back since that fateful day. I discussed with them the fact that I needed to come face-to-face with the events that occurred that day and that I needed some time to just stand near the building and confront my fears since it would be all too soon before I would have to return to work there.

I explained that 3,000 people had to be relocated. Some of us were supposed to be moved to NAVFAC in Building 33, many more in Building 201, and others going to various different buildings. I thought I was one of those heading to Building 33 so I asked one of the guards if he knew where Building 33 was. The other guard got out a map of the base and showed me where he thought Building 33 was located. I told him I'd heard it was supposed to be across from the William III coffee shop so we should look for a building that has a large cafe directly opposite it. There was another office complex, Building 108 that also had a building directly opposite a little courtyard-looking area, so I kept that in mind too. The guard said we could go up the adjacent street to Building 33 then go through the parking garage in order to circle around a one way street, and then come past the front gate guards and arrive at Building 108. We drove as instructed, but after driving past Building 33 and Building 108, we determined Building 108 couldn't be the right place because the courtyard space looked too narrow for people to walk through.

After visiting Building 108, we returned to the garage. Since I knew he wouldn't be back up here any time soon, I showed my husband where the van from my vanpool parks. He parked the car in that van parking spot because it was on the same level as the entrance to Building 197. Then he got out of the car and came around to my side to help me out of the car. He took me by my hand and we walked toward the exit of the garage facing Building 197. I was really tentative about approaching Building 197, so my husband put his arm around me. He's not a very demonstrative individual, but he half guided, half dragged me out of the garage and across the street to the fence. We stopped for a few minutes so I could compose myself. He asked me if that was the door I use. I explained the hours people were allowed to use this doorway closer to the north side of the building. After a few minutes, we continued to walk up to the fence surrounding Building 197 and my husband reached out and touched the cloth on the fence. He touched it to show me it was only material. He lifted one of the window flaps in the fence covering and told me to look in. Then he told me to touch the fence cover material. He urged me on and I lifted my hand and slowly moved it forward until my fingers touched the material. I hesitated for a few more minutes and then brushed my fingers against the opaque fence covering. Then my husband had me spend more time with my hand touching that material. Soon I had my hand resting on the fencing covering.

When I touched the material, I didn't feel anything. No angst, no fear, no palpitations in my heart; nothing. It was just like reaching out and touching a normal fence with protective cloth on it. I didn't lift the cloth window vent to look in, but did look in when my husband opened it for me. I observed a lot of mildew accumulating on the ceiling of the porch foyer where I hadn't noticed any when I was actively using that entrance. Tears were rolling down my face, but I didn't know why since I didn't feel anything.

We were arm in arm and preparing to leave the sidewalk in front of Building 197 when Master Chief Elben drove up to us and stopped his car to say hello. He asked if this was my first time back and I told him it was. He asked if I'd talked to Nina lately. I replyed I'd talked to her, but not lately. I told him I owed her a phone call. He then recommended that where we were standing was a good place to get settled and that we should stay right there. Then he told my husband to hold me tight. I had to translate that for my husband because he's hard of hearing. So, I told him what the Master Chief said and made him put both arms around me. Master Chief smiled, then said goodby and drove off.

After a few minutes I felt well enough to walk back across the street and get back into the car. I asked my husband to drive slowly past the building so I could spend more time making sense of it all. He drove slowly and then we left the base. Since I did so well, we went shopping at Ft. Belvoir to finish off the day before going home.

The visit to the Navy Yard was the first really big step in my healing process and it wasn't easy. I continue seeing a psychiatrist, and two psychologists; one specializing in Mind and Body and the other in Eye Movement Desensitization Redirection (EMDR). We had a Chaplain's group therapy group going for a while, and I was seeing a Therapist until I began seeing the two Psychologists. There is always homework to do, and always the constant battle with my thoughts. Some of my own thoughts have dropped off along the way and with the help of these many therapists, I am managing to slowly master my demons.

My healing continues, slowly, and, of course, still not fast enough for my liking. I'm impatient, and I know it. I find out from others who are going through the same thing that time heals, and with time, I realize I will heal too. The visit to the Navy Yard was just the first step in my healing process. This book is another step of my healing process. There will be more steps in the future; little steps and big ones. Each will come together to help me toward my own healing. I hope others will find their path toward their healing also. The person I become when all is said and done will be better for having gone through the experience and come out on the other side. Love and hugs to all who have helped me get even this far.

GLOSSARY

A

Adjacent cubicles – cubicles located next to each other with a cloth on metal frame, and no space separating them.

Alarm – a constant sound, either wavering or pulsing indicating a problem in the building, notifying occupants to prepare for directions for egress.

Atrium – open area from the first floor to second or more floors allowing a view to the first floor from the upper floors.

B

BUMED – Bureau of Medicine

C

CAC – Common Access Card-used to gain entrance to the building and computer at work.

CEAP – Civilian Employee Assistance Program, a program paid for by NAVSEA to provide assistance to employees experiencing difficulties in a number of areas

CNIC- Navy Installations Command. Responsible for worldwide shore installation support for the U. S. Navy under the Chief of Naval Operations (CNO). Mission is to support the three F's: Fleet, Fighter, and Family.

Commuter lot – A lot not far off of I-95 where commuters park and catch either a ride, bus or van to continue their commute to workplaces in the DC, North VA, or South MD areas

Contractor (delivery) – A non-seated contractor designated to develop or deliver a product

Contractor (seated) – A person with a computer and phone assigned to him or her because that is the spot he or she is to report to work to perform duties for the government

Corpsman – A Navy term used to describe an enlisted person who has had medical technician training and can provide minor medical assistance in the case of emergencies

Cranes – Types of machines, generally equipped with a hoist, wire ropes or chains, and sheaves, that can be used both to lift and lower heavy materials during the building process and to move them horizontally.

D

Defense Security Service (DSS) – The service responsible for processing secret and top secret clearances as employees are hired in the Department of Defense

E

ERP – Enterprise Resource Planning, of which NAVSEA is using the finance and timekeeping portions to manage budgets

F

FBI – Federal Bureau of Investigation

Free-standing part of desk – part of desktop that juts into the middle of the office and is supported by a leg on the extreme outside end.

G

Girders- steel horizontal or angular supports in a building

GoPhone- a pay as you use it phone, usually purchased for disposable use.

GPS - Global Positioning System.

Gun control - a pet agenda pushed for at the memorial for the fallen of the Navy Yard shootings by two speakers.

H

HOV-3 - The delineation for the HOV lanes around the Washington DC beltway and roads South requiring 3 people in a vehicle to make use of the HOV lanes during rush hour traffic.

I

Intern program - The program that develops new employees with the purpose of allowing them to proceed up the ranks by means of achieving ever more increasing roles with responsibility over a period of several years.

Instructions - The method used by the Navy to regulate processes, assigned numerical numbering by the subject matter covered.

J

K

L

Linear thinking - The method of problem solving that attacks the problem linearly instead of using a matrix method of thinking.

Lower bookshelf - the cubicles in our office area contained a lower bookshelf upon which we placed the books less used. This is the bookshelf that would have fallen had I bumped it just the wrong way when I changed position.

M

Maritime Plaza - The building at the end of M Street that had a large parking lot of which we took advantage for the memorial serivce.

Marine Barracks - A well-guarded and fenced in area in the middle of the DC area and very close to the Navy Yard with space enough for the Memorial service.

Muster list - The list everyone must sign when entering an evacuation site, the purpose of which is to track those who are in each building and who haven't yet left the affected building.

N

NAVFAC - Naval Facilities Command

NAVSEA - Naval Sea Systems Command

NCIS - Naval Community Investigaive Serivce

New normal - The new situation we were experiencing was what the group therapy instructors called our new normal and would remain so for the next several months.

O

P

Pallor - A coloring in the inside atmosphere that made the air look gray-blue and sickly, if air can indeed look that way.

Periscope - an attachment on a submarine that is raised to the surface to view occurances above the water.

Policy Letter is a stop-gap measure to provide guidance specifically for funding of academic degrees until the Instruction can be updated and signed.

PTSD - Post Traumatic Stress Disorder, an effect of sudden emergency experiences faced by some people who aren't prepared to work through it.

Q

R

Red Cross - a volunteer organization brought into service for emergencies both abroad and at home.

S

Sanctuary - A place were people are made to feel safe after having been in harm's way.

SEA-10 family - Within NAVSEA, there are several organizations. The SEA10 organization is a part of the HQ group and contains mostly people of the HR job series. Our department falls within the SEA 10 group, which we tend to call a family.

Security clearance - Before working in our building, one must have at least a secret security clearance; meaning, be cleared by Defense Security Service with at least an interim clearance.

Sixteen (16) inch guns - The largest guns afixed to the battleship decking that would be bombarding the shoreline during WWII.

Systemic - Affecting a group or system, such as a body, economy, market or society as a whole.

T

U

Ubercars - a unique car company in the DC area that matches drivers and cars and at an extremely competitive rate.

V

Vertical file – a file cabinet that holds contents along the front of the drawers instead of going back into the drawer, or holds two rows of contents in a shallow drawer.

W

Webbed chair - An ergonoically designed chair finished with webbed fabric instead of the usual padding and upholstery.

Wounded Warrior - classification for a prior service member who was wounded while on active duty with at least a 10% disability and is afforded special hiring because of this status.

X

Y

Z

Made in the USA
Lexington, KY
29 June 2015